RISK TRENDS OF U.S. MULTINATIONAL AND DOMESTIC FIRMS

RISK TRENDS OF U.S. MULTINATIONAL AND DOMESTIC FIRMS

Mehmet Yasar Geyikdagi

PRAEGER

PRAEGER SPECIAL STUDIES • PRAEGER SCIENTIFIC

Library of Congress Cataloging in Publication Data

Geyikdagi, Mehmet Yasar.
  Risk trends of U.S. multinational and domestic firms.

  Bibliography: p.
  Includes index.
  1. Risk—United States. 2. Capital investments
—United States. 3. Business enterprises—United
States. 4. Corporations, American. I. Title.
II. Title: Risk trends of U.S. multi-
national and domestic firms.
HD61.G49   1982   338.7'4'0973   82-10155
ISBN 0-03-061924-6

Published in I982 by Praeger Publishers
CBS Educational and Professional Publishing
A Division of CBS, Inc.
521 Fifth Avenue, New York, New York 10175 U.S.A.

© 1982 by Praeger Publishers

23456789 052 987654321
Printed in the United States of America

Preface

This study tests the hypothesis that the cost of equity capital and hence the total risk of U.S. multinational firms would decrease in relation to that of U.S. domestic firms because of the maturing attitudes of both the host countries and the multinational corporations, as well as the improvement of communications.

It has been found that between 1965 and 1978, host countries, which are recipients of foreign direct investment, have adopted a more mature and sophisticated attitude vis-a-vis the multinational firms. They have specified the type of foreign direct investment they sought more clearly and made appropriate rules more specific and clear. Likewise, the multinational firms have become more mature, experienced, and sophisticated in their relationships with host countries. Moreover, communications have shown major improvements during the same period.

The results of the tests conducted by the author are generally supportive of the above hypothesis. The cost of equity capital and the earnings-price for the overall averages of U.S. multinational firms have decreased in relation to that of U.S. domestic firms during the period from 1965 to 1978. This means that the total risk of the multinational firms decreased in relation to that of the domestic firms. Systematic risk, as measured by beta values, has been roughly the same for both between 1971 and 1973. After that, the beta average of the domestic firms decreased in relation to that of the multinationals because of the synchronism of economic cycles in major Western industrialized countries.

Acknowledgments

First of all, I would like to express my deep appreciation to Professor Cyril R. Tomkins of the University of Bath in England, who has so significantly contributed to the development of ideas and the proper methodology in this study. Throughout the entire preparation period, his comments and suggestions have been most valuable.

I also owe much to my wife, Nejla Geyikdagi, who not only assisted me with lengthy data collection and computations, but also verified my statistical methodology and made comments throughout the text.

I also wish to emphasize the help provided by librarians at the University of Bath, Harvard University, Columbia University, and the University of Montreal.

Obviously, I bear the responsibility for this study, and any shortcomings are mine.

Contents

RISK TRENDS OF
U.S. MULTINATIONAL AND
DOMESTIC FIRMS

1

Introduction

PURPOSE OF THE STUDY

The purpose of this study is to compare the cost of equity capital and total risk of U.S. multinational firms with that of U.S. domestic firms during the 1965-78 period and then to analyze and evaluate the research findings in terms of their application to business and investment decision making.

RESEARCH QUESTIONS

It will be shown that the host countries are adopting a more mature and sophisticated attitude vis-a-vis the multinationals and vice-versa and that communications and transportation have vastly improved. It is hypothesized that these factors will tend to reduce the risk of U.S. multinational firms as perceived by U.S. stockholders in comparison to that of U.S. domestic firms. Hence, an empirical test will be carried out to see whether or not this really is the case.

A survey of the literature shows that virtually no research at all has been made in this area. The only empirical studies that compare the costs of equity capital of multinational and domestic firms are those of Theodor Kohers (1971; 1975) and Aggarwal (1979). According to Geyikdagi (1980), such studies offer no possibilities of establishing trends, let alone finding the factors behind these trends. The dearth of empirical studies on multinationals certainly does not help companies and other investors who would like to make sound investment decisions. This becomes even more important when the direct investments of U.S. multinational corporations have attained

1

so large a magnitude. Hence, this study should prove of importance to U.S. investors as well as to host countries. Accordingly, the following brief background information is relevant at this point.

Today, there is virtual unanimity that U.S. multinational corporations play a very important part in the U.S. as well as in the world economy. According to Kohers (1971; p. 2), the foreign operations of U.S. companies are essential in transmitting knowledge, technology, administration, and resources not only to other countries but also by way of feedback to the United States. By combining their own techniques with those available in the host countries, the multinationals attain a new synthesis and the process may repeat itself.

U.S. foreign private direct investments have reached a very high level. They were estimated at $70 billion in 1969 and according to Kozlow, Rutter, and Walker (1978, p. 16), they reached $148.8 billion in 1977. During the 1960s, plant and equipment expenditures of U.S. subsidiaries abroad have grown twice as fast as those for domestic affiliates. During the same period, the annual return of earnings from these foreign investments exceeded the yearly direct investment outflows for the past ten years (Kohers 1971, p. 3). Sales by majority-owned foreign affiliates of U.S. companies increased from $108.5 billion in 1967 to $514.7 billion in 1976 (Chung 1978, p. 32). Even though these figures are not adjusted for constant dollars, the growth is still very considerable.

The reason for starting our analysis in 1965 is that there was not a sufficient number of multinational firms before that year (Kohers 1971, pp. 65-66). The reason for taking the multinational corporations of the United States rather than some other country is that the United States is not only by far the largest foreign direct investor in the world, but is also the only country to have a large enough sample of large domestic firms and large multinational firms that could be compared. The sample has been selected from "The Fortune Top 500 Firms" listed on the New York Stock Exchange. The author of this study attempted to carry out the same type of analysis with companies of the United Kingdom, which is second in the world in foreign private direct investment, but could not get a significant sample. Firms that have 30 percent (35 percent after 1974) or more of their operations abroad are defined as multinationals, whereas firms with 10 percent (15 percent after 1974) or less of foreign operations are domestics. Although these cutoff rates have an element of arbitrariness, widening the difference between them would have greatly reduced the number of firms in the sample. On the other hand, narrowing the difference would have cast serious doubts as to whether two different types of firms, multinationals and domestics, are really being compared. More explanations about the implications of these cutoff rates will be given in Chapter 3.

To measure risk, we shall use earnings-price ratios, the cost of equity capital (the Gordon dividend valuation model), and the betas of the capital asset pricing model. Subsequently we shall explain in greater detail the reasoning and implications behind the selection of these criteria. We shall see how the average risks of the sample of 28 multinational firms we take compare year by year with their domestic counterparts, which also total 28 firms, during the 1965-78 period. Other things being equal, the higher the earnings-price ratios or the costs of equity capital, the higher the total risk will be. The betas, on the other hand, will measure systematic risk, which is only a part of total company risk. Naturally a lower total risk for a firm will mean lower costs of equity and debt capital and hence a lower weighted average cost of capital. This is important both for the investor and the corporate manager as well as for the host country, which wants foreign private investment on the most suitable financial terms. All of them would find it useful to know what the risk trends look like in the 1965-78 period and what major factors lie behind these trends.

LIMITATIONS OF THE STUDY

A sample of 28 U.S. multinational firms and 28 U.S. domestic firms is substantial, yet a larger sample would, of course, have been better. The same could be said for the number of years encompassed by the study. Instead of the 14 years that we studied, a longer period would certainly have been preferable. However, as we shall explain in Chapter 3, which deals with the methodology, we found that a larger sample and a longer period were impossibilities.

Another point is that the formulas and models used in our study are based on certain assumptions like constant growth rates for firms or perfect markets. It is quite unlikely that these assumptions are fully valid in the real world. However, since our study is basically one of comparing two samples, namely the multinationals and the domestic, any method of computation that tends to slant the values in one sample is likely to do the same for the other sample. Moreover, because of the substantial number of firms in each sample, the law of large numbers should work to our advantage.

NATURE AND ORDER OF PRESENTATION

This volume begins with an explanation of the evolution and importance of multinational business to the world and the United States. Then the methodology used in the study will be described. Afterward, we will deal with the maturing of the multinational firms and the host countries along with a short discussion of the improvement in communications that tends to facilitate multinational business. An empirical (statistical) test will then be carried out, and its results will be interpreted and analyzed. Making use of the results, we will analyze each industry group separately and then compare forward-looking and historical growth rates, which are used in calculating the cost of equity capital. Theories of international business and how they relate to our findings will also be examined. Finally, of course, a conclusion will be stated. In the appendix, major economic events during the 1965-78 period are reviewed.

2

The Evolution of
Multinational Business:
Its Significance and Meaning

Companies that operate in more than one country do not constitute a novelty. Various Indian companies, the most prominent of which was the British East India Company, or the merchant bankers of London or the Rothschilds, who, being established in five different European countries, made transfers to one another and owned mining interests in countries where they were not represented; Spanish mercury mines were one example. Toward the end of the nineteenth century or at the beginning of the twentieth century, U.S. companies like International Harvester, Singer, Standard Oil, and Ford established themselves and produced in several countries abroad, just as British, Swiss, and Dutch companies did. There is the problem of defining these firms either as international or as multinational, the latter gaining widespread usage only in the 1960s (Leon 1977, p. 499).

Several definitions have been proposed. According to one definition, any firm, which has more than 25 percent of its sales abroad, is considered a multinational. Until World War II, it could not be conceived that a firm could make more than 5 or 10 percent of its sales abroad. In 1970, more than 100 U.S. companies had more than 25 percent of their sales abroad. Another definition makes use of a firm's percentage of investments that are abroad. Other definitions or criteria include being listed on more than one financial market, the percentage of employees outside the home country, or the percentage of total investments that is overseas (Leon 1977, pp. 499-500). The criterion of sales seems to be by far the most widespread one in the literature.

Besides the above criteria, a multinational firm has a management that is differentiated because of its operations on several markets. The subsidiary abroad is not regarded as a poor relative but as an equal, which has a lot of autonomy and must be reckoned with. This distinguishes it from the traditional international firm where the subsidiary has little to say in the central board. In contrast to international firms, multinational corporations use foreigners even at the highest levels of the company. For example, the president of IBM is Jacques Maisonrouge, a Frenchman. Actually, the multinational corporation is still a new phenomenon, which does not conform to a unique model or organization (Leon 1977, p. 502). It is still in the trial-and-error or, perhaps, soul-searching stage. That, in a sense, may be helpful since it would give the multinational firm ample opportunity for maneuver and adaptation when it faces changing circumstances in the world. In other words, it is still malleable enough to adapt to new conditions and to mature, as we shall see later.

The United Nations uses the term transnational rather than multinational on the grounds that the former is more descriptive of the concept of a parent firm based in one country with operating affiliates in a number of foreign countries. The term multinational would then denote a company owned by several nationalities, whether or not it had affiliates in other countries. Actually, the preference for transnational is not merely technical but rests on the belief that the term more accurately reflects the quality of domination inherent in the parent-subsidiary relationship in contrast with the implication of coequality in multinational. Notwithstanding these distinctions, the word multinational will encompass both multinationals and transnationals in this study.

Major factors that lead U.S. companies to set up or increase manufacturing facilities abroad include the following (Fatemi, de Saint-Phalle, and Keefe 1963, p. 163; U.S. Department of Commerce 1972, p. 14):

Tariffs, import quotas, and currency controls, which, of course, limit exports.

Lower transportation costs on goods produced locally in the host countries.

Saturated markets in the United States.

Expectation of higher profits in economies with a growth rate higher than that of the United States.

Patent laws that, in certain countries, require firms to manufacture locally in order to obtain patent protection.

Foreign consumer preference for simpler and cheaper versions of certain goods produced and sold in the United States.

Lower corporation income taxes and more generous depreciation allowances in certain countries; in some cases, tax holidays and other financial inducements.

International versus domestic diversification.

Antitrust laws in the United States.

In the late 1950s, the Eisenhower administration thought that the main forces that led U.S. corporations to invest abroad were stability, security, and the quest for profit. Protection of the actual or potential market against Western Europe or Japan was another factor. Great efforts were made to create a suitable investment climate in the world and to convince investors of good returns on investment with a reasonable payback period. Many corporations with international orientations made use of this opportunity to develop their operations abroad (U.S. Department of Commerce 1972, p. 14).

Multinational business, mainly resulting from foreign direct investment, has become more important than foreign trade as the main agent of international economic relations in terms of size, rate of growth, and future potential.

> Following World War II, Western Europe, and many nations in Latin America, Asia and Africa welcomed investments from abroad of almost any kind. The multinational corporation broke through the walls of the nation state. The International Monetary Fund, the International Bank for Reconstruction and Development, the General Agreement on Tariffs and Trade, the Organization for Economic Cooperation and Development and the United Nations Conference for Trade and Development have all advocated the liberalization of capital. . . . Over the last two decades the concurrent growth of the multinational corporations and rise of nationalism in many countries have brought to the fore conflicting schools of thought that rest on varying assumptions and conclusions as to what determines the massive growth of international investment and what course it is likely to follow (Fatemi, Williams, and de Saint-Phalle 1976, pp. 14, 41).

For example, while one person may argue that the total risk for multinational firms has been continually rising during the last decade, another individual may claim just the opposite. This arises mainly from the dearth of empirical studies on multinational business and related topics.

In 1977 the book value of U.S. direct investments rose to $148.7 billion. This figure excludes long-term investments in stocks and bonds. Another important aspect of the multinational firm is that net foreign investment income since 1968 has been much greater than net receipts from the trade account. In 1960, there was a $4.9 billion net balance on the trade account and a $.5 billion net balance on the direct foreign investment account. In 1970, the export surplus from trade fell to $2.1 billion, which is less than the $3.5 billion net income from investments abroad (Fatemi, Williams, and de Saint-Phalle 1976, p. 48). This difference grew even further as foreign investment income increased while the foreign trade surplus turned into a deficit. A look at Table 2.1 shows the increase in book value of U.S. direct private investment as well as its distribution throughout the world in 1960, 1965, 1973, and 1977.

TABLE 2.1. Location of U.S. Private Direct Investment in the World (in billions of dollars)

	1960	1965	1973	1977
Western Europe	6.7	14.0	37.2	60.6
percent	21.0	28.0	34.7	40.7
Canada	11.2	15.3	28.1	35.4
percent	35.0	31.0	26.2	23.8
Latin America	8.3	10.9	18.5	27.7
percent	26.0	22.0	17.2	18.6
Japan	0.3	0.7	2.7	4.1
percent	1.0	1.0	2.5	2.8
Other	5.4	8.6	20.8	20.9
percent	17.0	18.0	19.4	14.1
Total	31.9	49.5	107.3	148.7
percent	100.0	100.0	100.0	100.0

Note: Dollar figures have been converted into percentages to facilitate comparisons.

Source: Friedlin, N.J., and L.A. Lupo. November 1972. "U.S. Direct Investments Abroad in 1971." Survey of Current Business 52: 21-34; Lupo, L.A., September 1973. "U.S. Direct Investment Abroad in 1972." Ibid., 53: 21-34; Scholl, R.B., August 1974. "The International Investment Position of the United States: Developments in 1973." Ibid., 54: 1-6; Kozlow, R., J. Rutter, and P. Walker, August 1978. "U.S. Direct Investment Abroad in 1977." Ibid., 58: 16-38.

It can be seen from the table that the U.S. private direct investments abroad have shown the largest growth in Western Europe. The billion dollar figures for 1960, 1965, 1973, and 1977 are respectively 6.7, 14.0, 37.2, and 60.6. The share of Western Europe in the world has continuously risen. It was 21.0 percent in 1960, 28.0 percent in 1965, 34.7 percent in 1973, and 40.7 percent in 1977. Canada's share has fallen from 35.0 percent in 1960 to 23.8 percent in 1977. Latin America shows a decline from 26.0 percent in 1960 to 17.2 percent in 1973, then it rises slightly to 18.6 percent in 1977. Although Canada's share declined, it still continues to be by far the largest single recipient of U.S. investment. The fact that Japan's share has remained quite low is due to the restrictions imposed by Japan rather than a lack of interest by U.S. corporations. These restrictions emanate from a worry of U.S. control of Japanese business as well as the very different employment practices of the United States as compared with Japan (Fatemi, Williams, and de Saint-Phalle 1976, pp. 49-59).

Figures for the 1971 and 1977 U.S. direct investment by industry groups are shown in Table 2.2. It can be seen that while the share of oil has declined between 1971 and 1977, the shares of both manufacturing and particularly other industries have gained prominence during the same period.

TABLE 2.2. U.S. Private Direct Investment by Industry Groups (in billions of dollars)

Industry Group	1971	1977
Petroleum	24.2	30.8
percent	28.1	20.7
Manufacturing	35.6	65.6
percent	41.3	44.1
Other industries	26.4	52.3
percent	30.6	35.1

Source: Lupo, L.A., September 1973. "U.S. Direct Investment Abroad in 1972." Survey of Current Business 53: 26-27; Kozlow, R., J. Rutter, and P. Walker, August 1978. "U.S. Direct Investment Abroad in 1977." Ibid., 58: 16-48.

Sales by majority-owned foreign affiliates of U.S. companies by industry and by geographical area from 1967 to 1976 are shown in Table 2.3. It shows that sales in current dollars have increased from $108.5 billion in 1967 to $514.7 billion in 1976. Except for mining and smelting, all industries have grown at a very substantial rate during the ten-year period. When we examine the sales in specific areas, we see that the developed countries accounted for almost three-quarters of the total sales until 1974, when speedily increasing oil prices brought the share of developed countries down to less than two-thirds of the total. This is understandable since the greater part of the oil is sold by U.S. affiliates located in developed countries like Saudi Arabia, Libya, Nigeria, Venezuela, Indonesia, etc.

TABLE 2.3. Sales by Majority-owned Foreign Affiliates of U.S. Companies – 1967-76
(in billions of dollars)

	1967	1968	1969	1970	1971
Total	108.5	120.8	134.3	155.9	184.4
By industry					
Mining and smelting	3.5	3.9	4.2	4.5	3.9
Petroleum	31.1	34.0	36.4	42.4	53.1
Manufacturing	52.6	59.6	67.6	78.3	90.9
Food products	6.1	6.2	6.8	7.5	9.1
Paper and allied products	2.0	2.6	3.0	3.4	4.2
Chemicals and allied products	8.5	9.8	11.0	12.6	15.0
Rubber products	1.8	1.9	2.2	2.4	2.7
Primary and fabricated metals	4.6	5.3	6.0	7.6	6.7
Nonelectrical machinery	7.6	8.6	10.2	12.3	14.3
Electrical machinery	4.6	5.1	5.9	7.7	9.1
Transportation equipment	12.1	14.2	16.1	16.8	20.4
Other	5.4	5.9	6.4	8.0	9.4
Trade	14.5	16.2	18.3	21.6	25.4
Other industries	6.9	7.0	7.7	9.0	11.1
By area					
Total developed (percent)	73	72	74	74	75
Developed countries	79.2	88.0	98.5	116.2	136.3
Canada	26.8	29.8	32.3	35.1	40.3
Europe	44.2	49.1	55.8	68.4	81.2
European communities(9)*	37.5	41.2	46.6	57.6	68.4
France	5.5	6.5	7.4	8.3	10.5
Germany	8.1	8.8	10.6	14.6	17.1
United Kingdom	14.7	15.1	16.2	18.5	21.6
Other	9.2	10.7	12.4	16.2	19.1
Other Europe	6.7	7.9	9.2	10.9	12.8
Japan	2.5	2.9	3.4	4.2	5.1
Australia, New Zealand, and South Africa	5.6	6.2	7.0	8.5	9.7
Total developing (percent)	27	28	26	26	26
Developing countries	25.9	29.2	32.2	35.1	41.8
Latin America	15.8	17.4	18.8	20.1	21.4
Other Africa	2.3	2.8	3.2	3.6	4.1
Middle East	4.2	4.7	5.3	5.8	8.9
Other Asia and Pacific	3.7	4.3	4.9	5.7	7.5
International and unallocated	3.4	3.6	3.6	4.6	6.3

	1972	1973	1974	1975	1976
Total	211.9	291.4	437.7	463.1	514.7
By industry					
Mining and smelting	3.2	4.0	5.1	4.6	5.5
Petroleum	58.8	90.8	184.9	183.5	205.5
Manufacturing	107.6	140.9	175.7	192.3	212.8
Food products	10.4	13.7	17.0	18.3	20.4
Paper and allied products	5.2	7.0	9.3	9.2	10.1
Chemicals and allied products	17.8	25.5	36.2	37.6	43.1
Rubber products	3.2	3.9	5.0	5.4	5.7
Primary and fabricated metals	7.6	9.5	12.5	12.6	14.4
Nonelectrical machinery	17.0	22.2	27.4	32.1	34.2
Electrical machinery	10.8	13.9	17.4	18.8	18.4
Transportation equipment	24.4	30.3	32.7	38.1	44.8
Other	11.2	14.9	18.2	20.2	21.7
Trade	30.1	38.9	46.1	52.2	58.0
Other industries	12.2	16.9	25.9	30.6	33.0
By area					
Total developed (percent)	75	71	62	65	66
Developed countries	158.2	207.8	272.2	302.8	337.3
Canada	45.0	56.5	71.4	78.5	89.0
Europe	95.9	127.3	165.8	186.5	206.7
European communities(9)*	80.7	107.0	138.5	155.8	171.5
France	13.1	17.7	22.1	26.1	26.7
Germany	20.5	28.9	34.6	38.1	44.3
United Kingdom	24.5	30.2	40.6	45.9	48.6
Other	22.5	30.2	41.6	45.7	51.9
Other Europe	15.2	20.3	27.2	30.7	35.2
Japan	6.7	10.0	16.8	17.8	20.1
Australia, New Zealand, and South Africa	10.6	14.1	18.2	20.1	21.5
Total developing (percent)	25	29	38	35	34
Developing countries	47.9	74.0	148.3	146.6	163.9
Latin America	23.7	33.3	51.6	57.3	60.6
Other Africa	4.5	6.0	10.1	10.2	13.2
Middle East	11.1	22.2	64.1	57.4	66.5
Other Asia and Pacific	8.6	12.5	22.5	21.7	23.6
International and unallocated	5.8	9.6	17.2	13.7	13.5

*The European Communities (9) were established in 1973. Estimates for earlier years are the sum of estimates for the European Communities (6), Denmark, Ireland, and the United Kingdom.
Source: Kozlow, Rutter, and Walker 1978, p. 32.

11

3

Methodology

As already mentioned, the purpose of this study is to compare the total risk of U.S. multinational corporations with that of U.S. domestic firms during a specific period (1965-78).

Our hypothesis is that the total risk of U.S. multinational corporations, as shown by their cost of equity capital or their earnings-price ratio, has decreased in relation to that of domestic firms. We assume that the factors leading to such a relative decrease in the risk of multinationals arise from the maturing attitudes of both the host countries and the multinational firms themselves. Moreover, it is assumed that improvements in communications had positive effects toward decreasing the risk of operating abroad. These factors will be explained in detail in the next chapter, which will primarily attempt to show the increasingly sophisticated attitude of the host countries toward the multinational firm. After that, the tests will be presented, which will attempt to check out the validity of our hypothesis. We will also analyse the results and produce extensions. The rest of this chapter will explain how the sample of firms used in the tests was selected, which methods are used to measure risk, and which statistical techniques are used and why.

The reason for taking 28 multinationals and 28 domestics is that this was the maximum number of industrial firms that could be selected within the constraints of a minimum size for all the firms in the sample, a maximum multinationality for the domestics and a minimum multinationality for the multinationals. The main reason for selecting industrial firms is to have a greater degree of homogeneity in the sample. Accordingly, only those firms were selected that were among the Fortune directory of the top 500 largest U.S. industrial corporations. Of these corporations, those that had only 10 percent or less of their sales abroad were defined as domestics, and those having 30 percent or more were accepted as multinationals. As can be expected, the average sales abroad of the multinationals in the sample will be above 30 percent, and that of the average domestic will be less than 10 percent. After 1974, due to increasing foreign content in many large U.S. firms, a norm was established at 15 percent or less for domestic firms and 35 percent or more for multinational firms. The average difference, of course, was far larger than 20 percentage points. The degree of multi-nationality of each firm has been established from various studies (Bruck and Lees 1968; Fatemi, Williams, and de Saint-Phalle 1976, pp. 301-11; Kohers 1971, pp. 30-11; Value Line Investment Survey) already carried out as well as the reports of the companies themselves. In addition, some of the companies were contacted directly when necessary. The number of domestic and multinational firms in each Standard Industrial Classification group is shown in Table 3.1.

TABLE 3.1. Distribution of Firms in the Sample

Industry Group	SIC Code	No. Firms/Group	
		Multinational	Domestic
Petroleum refining	291	3	3
Electrical machinery	3	3	3
Nonelectrical machinery	35	8	3
Chemical and allied products	28	7	5
Fabricated metal products	34	2	5
Nonferrous metals	333	2	3
Food products	20	3	6
All groups lumped together		28	28

INVESTOR'S SELECTION OF STOCK AND THE EVALUATION OF RISK

Our reasoning will be based on the premise that there is a trade-off between risk and return. The higher the risk, the higher will be the return required by the investor to compensate for that risk. Likewise, the lower the risk, the lower the required rate of return will be.

Three measures of risk will be used: (1) the earnings-price ratio (earnings yield); (2) the cost of equity capital based on the dividend valuation model; and (3) the systematic risk as measured by the beta of the capital asset pricing model. An examination of each method follows.

The Earnings-Price Ratio

The earnings-price ratio or earnings yield is simply the reciprocal of the price-earnings ratio, which is apparently the most widely used stock evaluation method in the world of investment. Simply defined, the price-earnings ratio is the average price during a year divided by earnings during the same year.

The reason why we prefer to use the earnings-price ratio rather than its more frequently employed reciprocal, the price-earnings ratio, is to make clearer and more direct comparisons with the cost of equity capital and the betas, both of which are assumed to increase when risk increases. Obviously, the reverse is true for a multiple like the price-earnings ratio, which is assumed to vary inversely with risk.

Accordingly, a strong, successful, and promising company tends to sell at a higher price-earnings ratio (consequently at a lower earnings-price ratio) than a weaker, less promising, and less successful one (Graham, Dodd, and Cottle 1962, p. 230).

The main factors influencing the price-earnings (or the earnings-price) ratio may be the following (Graham, Dodd, and Cottle 1962, p. 230):

Those factors that are fully reflected in the financial data (tangible factors) are: (a) growth of earnings and past sales; (b) profitability; (c) stability of past earnings; (d) the dividend rate and record; and (e) financial strength, or credit standing.

These factors that are not reflected openly in the data (intangible factors) are: (a) quality of management; (b) nature and prospects of the industry; and (c) competitive position and individual prospects of the firm.

The above factors indicate that the price-earnings ratio or its inverse, the earnings-price ratio, reflects to a great extent the judgment of a firm by the market.

According to Amling (1978), the significance of the price-earnings ratio is related to the expectations of investors about future earnings of the firm. Investors will pay more for a current dollar of earnings if they expect earnings to increase substantially in the future. Hence, a firm that promises to have a future growth of earnings will sell at a higher price-earnings ratio, and one with expected declining earnings will sell at a low price-earnings ratio

(Amling; 1978: 471). As we assume that the majority of investors are averse to risk, the stability of earnings will influence the ratio. Hence, if a share's earnings have been unstable in the past and are expected to be unstable in the future as well, the market will tend to underprice it in relation to its earnings because of the instability. Hence, there will be a low price-earnings ratio and inversely a high earnings-price ratio (earnings yield). As mentioned above, the stability of earnings is not the only factor influencing a share's riskiness. Nonetheless, it is a very important factor.

For this study, the price-earnings figures, from which the earnings-price ratios are derived, have been taken from the Value Line Investment Survey, which defines them as the average annual prices of the stock divided by its annual earnings per share as reported by the company.

The Cost of Equity Capital Using the Dividend Valuation Model

The present price of a share of common stock depends upon (1) the cash flow investors expect to receive if they buy the stock and (2) the riskiness of these expected cash flows. The expected cash flow, in turn, is composed of two elements: (1) the dividend expected in each year and (2) the price investors expect to receive when they sell the stock at the end of the year (Weston and Brigham 1978, p. 639; Gordon 1962, pp. 46-47).

If a firm reinvests a constant proportion of its earnings and such reinvestments, on average, produce a given constant return, it can be accepted that dividends will grow at a constant rate.* The price P_0, of the share to the investor will be:

$$P_0 = \frac{D_1}{(1 + k_e)} + \frac{D_1(1 + g)}{(1 + k_e)^2} + \frac{D_1(1 + g)^2}{(1 + k_e)^3}$$

$$+ \ldots + \frac{D_1(1 + g)^t}{(1 + k_e)^{t+1}} + \ldots$$

where D_1 is the dividend at the end of the current period, which is assumed to have just started, k_e is the market capitalization rate or the cost of equity capital, and g is the growth rate of dividends. The above equation becomes:

$$P_0 = \frac{D_1}{(1 + k_e)} \left[1 + \frac{(1 + g)}{(1 + k_e)} + \left(\frac{1 + g}{1 + k_e} \right)^2 + \ldots \right]$$

*Under such an assumption, the growth rate of dividends would equal that of earnings.

The sum in the bracket is an infinite series. When simplified, it becomes:

$$1 + \left(\frac{1 + g}{1 + k_e}\right) + \left(\frac{1 + g}{1 + k_e}\right)^2 + \cdots$$

$$= \frac{1}{1 - (1 + g)/(1 + k_e)} = \frac{1 + k_e}{k_e - g}$$

Inserting it in the equation above, we have:

$$P_0 = \left(\frac{D_1}{1 + k_e}\right)\left(\frac{1 + k_e}{k_e - g}\right) = \frac{D_1}{k_e - g}$$

from which the cost of equity capital is derived as:

$$k_e = \frac{D_1}{P_0} + g$$

In this research, k_e will be calculated in two ways. First, it will be calculated in the same way as Kohers (1975, p. 122) did. D_1/P_0 is obtained by adding up the dividends per share in quarters 1 through 4 and dividing the total by the market price per share in quarter 1. The same procedure is used for the next quarter, except that the dividends per share for quarter 1 are dropped and those in quarter 5, added. In the denominator, the market price per share of quarter 2 is used.

The percentage change in dividends per share from one quarter to the next is taken as the growth rate g. Hence, the cost of equity capital of a particular company during the first two years will be:

1965/1 : D/P: $\frac{1965/1, 2, 3, 4}{1965/1}$ + % change in D

from 1965/1 to 1965/2

1965/2 : D/P: $\frac{1965/2, 3, 4, 1966/1}{1965/2}$ + % change in

D from 1965/2 to 1965/3

Secondly, k_e will be computed by adding the dividend yield to the expected future annual growth of cash flow earnings, both of which are taken from the Value Line Investment Survey. The dividend yield is the sum of the periodic dividend declarations during each year divided by the average annual price during the year. The cash flow earnings per share is defined as the net income plus noncash charges, which are chiefly depreciation, depletion, and amortization, minus preferred dividends (if any) divided by common shares outstanding at year end. The annual rates of change (growth) are calculated as a compounded annual rate of change from the latest three-year base period to the three-year period 3 to 5 years hence (Bernhard 1978, pp. 23, 34, 42).

These growth rates are estimated by the Value Line every year. They are ex ante or forward-looking. Hence, they may or may not be the same as the actual or ex post growth rates. For instance, the Value Line of 1965 may predict ex ante that the growth rate of a certain corporation will be 8 percent for the next three years. However, the ex post actual growth after three years may be less or more than the ex ante forward-looking Value Line estimated growth.

We believe that the second method not only reflects the investor's attitude better, since the Value Line is very widely used by investors, but it also makes growth forecasts that are based on a much longer base period in the past and extend further into the future. Hence, the interpretations will be based on the second method, and the first method will simply be a double check. This will be elaborated in Chapter 8.

Of course, the cost of equity capital, k_e, will contain a risk premium. Hence, if one firm's cost of equity capital is higher than another's, it is assumed that this is due to the higher risk associated with the first firm. Thus, a higher cost of equity capital will mean a higher risk, which is due to a risk-return trade-off.

The Betas of the Capital Asset Pricing Model

As mentioned before, the cost of equity capital of a share gives us the risk premium in addition to the risk-free rate. This risk premium corresponds to the total risk of a share. However, investors can diversify their securities to such an extent that the unsystematic risk, which is the risk particular to the share, will be eliminated, and the investors will be left with systematic risk, which is the risk pertaining to the market as a whole. In other words, by efficiently diversifying their portfolio of securities, investors can eliminate the unsystematic risk component of the shares, and then they will be left with only systematic risk. The beta is a measure of the sensitivity of a stock's price to overall market fluctuations. A beta of 1.50 indicates that a stock is likely to fluctuate 50 percent more than the general market in either direction.

Before elaborating upon the significance of the betas, the steps involved in computing a beta will be briefly discussed. First of all, a holding-period rate of return has to be found. A holding-period rate of return measures the total return investors could have realized had they held the asset during the period being studied (D'Ambrosio 1976, p. 346). Its formula would be:

$$r_{hp} = \frac{P_t - P_{t-1} + D_t}{P_{t-1}}$$

where r_{hp} is the holding-period rate of return; P_t is the ending price for the period in question; P_{t-1} is the beginning price for the period; and D_t is the cash received during total time.

Then the holding-period rates of return of both the individual asset and the market index, in which the asset is traded, are calculated. They are usually calculated weekly, biweekly, monthly, quarterly, etc., using no fewer than five years of data. The market index could be the Dow-Jones Industrial Average, the Standard and Poor's 500, the New York Stock Exchange Composite Index, etc., when one deals with U.S. firms (D'Ambrosio 1976, p. 347).

Next the characteristic line is computed. This line depicts the relationship between the rate of return on a single asset and the rate of return on the market for all assets (the market index). We take points, that is, the individual asset's return, the dependent variable on the ordinate and the return of the market, and the independent variable on the abscissa. The characteristic line is an ordinary least-squares regression line. The object is to minimize the sum of the squared deviations of the points from the regression (characteristic) line that graphs through the plot of all the observations. The beta is the slope of the regression (characteristic) line thus computed. Thus, the beta indicates the extent to which one can expect a change in the rate of return when the market's predicted rate of return is given. The greater the slope of a characteristic line is for a stock as depicted by its beta, the greater its systematic risk will be. The market beta will be equal to one (D'Ambrosio 1976, p. 334).

The betas in this study have been taken from the Value Line Investment Survey. Value Line betas use the New York Stock Exchange Composite Index as the measure of the market index (Bernhard 1978, pp. 10-12, 41-42). The individual asset's (stock's) rate of return and the New York Stock Exchange Composite Index rate of return are calculated weekly over a period of five years, and the beta is derived from a regression analysis as described above.

On average, betas explain about 30 percent of an individual stock's price changes. But for some stocks, the beta explains very little of the price fluctuations. Every stock has its own inherent

$$t = \frac{d - 0}{S_{d/\sqrt{n}}}$$

one finds the student's t value with (n - 1) degrees of freedom. The test with values of $\alpha \leq .20$ (.10 for each tail) will then be carried out. If $\alpha = .20$, there is an 80 percent confidence interval. The other values of α are .10, .05, .02, and .01. The lowest α value (highest confidence level) will be taken. Any t value that corresponds to an α value of less than .20 will be considered insignificant. Hence, a 95 percent confidence interval for the difference between the means would give

$$\bar{d} \pm t_{\alpha/2} \, S_d/\sqrt{n}$$

where $\alpha = .05$ or $t_{.025}$.

Thus, instead of testing for the equality of two sample means, the paired difference test examines n points in time. Such a block design increases the amount of information to be obtained.

The Standard Error around the Trend Line

The standard error of estimate around the trend line and the standard deviation are shown in the Figure 3.1. The standard error of estimate around the trend line consists of two lines that are parallel to the least-square trend (regression) line and have a vertical distance $S_{y.x}$ from it. In measuring stability, the standard error around the trend line will be used rather than the ordinary standard deviation, which is the pair of dashed lines parallel to the abscissa in Figure 3.1. The standard error around the trend line takes the trend of each group into account, while the standard deviation does not.

If the points are normally distributed around the regression line, it can be theoretically predicted that about 68 percent of the points will lie between the standard error around the trend lines.

The variance, which is the square of the standard deviation, may be calculated from the following relationship:

$$S^2 = \frac{\sum_{i=1}^{n} (Y_i - \bar{Y})^2}{n} \quad \text{and} \quad S = \sqrt{\frac{\sum_{i=1}^{n} (Y_i - \bar{Y})^2}{n}}$$

where S^2 is the variance, n is the number of observations, and $\bar{Y}$ is the mean of these observations. On the other hand, the formula for calculating the standard error around the trend line is:

$$\hat{S}^2 = \frac{\overset{n}{\underset{i=1}{\Sigma}}(Y_i - \hat{Y})^2}{n-2} \quad \text{and} \quad \hat{S} = \sqrt{\frac{\overset{n}{\underset{i=1}{\Sigma}}(Y_i - \hat{Y})^2}{n-2}}$$

where $\hat{S}$ is the standard error of estimate and $\hat{Y}_i$ are the predicted values of the observations. $\hat{Y}_i$ are the points lying on the trend line. These are explained in more detail by Spiegel (1961, p. 243) and Kohers (1971, pp. 90-94). It will also be shown how the computed values correlate with trend by computing the coefficient of correlation. To that end, the following equation will be used:

$$r = \sqrt{\frac{(Y_{est} - \bar{Y})^2}{(Y - \bar{Y})^2}}$$

where r is the coefficient of correlation between the estimated value of ¢ (Y_{est}), which lies on the trend line and the value of Y itself. $\bar{Y}$ is the mean value. This coefficient measures the temporal stability of the Y values, which are risk measures in the present study.

FIGURE 3.1. The Standard Error Around the Trend Line

Performance Variable

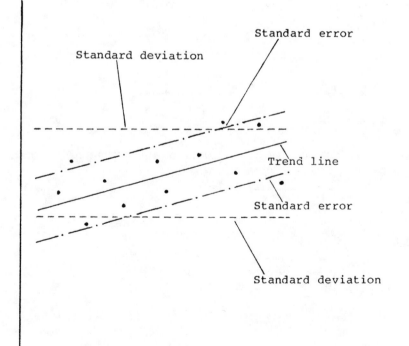

A Trend Significance Test

The third test aims at measuring the significance of the trend of the period-by-period differences between multinational corporations and domestic corporations as far as the costs of equity capital, the earnings-price ratios, and the betas are concerned. The differences are found by a procedure similar to that employed in the paired-difference test explained above.

Thus, there is a single distribution with a slope β_1. The hypothesis that $\beta_1 = 0$ should be tested against the alternative that $\beta_1 \neq 0$. The method of carrying out such a test is explained in detail by Mendenhall and Reinmuth (1974, pp. 333-36).

If $\beta_1 \neq 0$, then y and x can be linearly related. Here, y stands for any of the values such as the cost of equity capital, earnings-price ratios, and betas, while x represents the time periods. $\beta_1 \neq 0$ implies that a one unit change in x should bring about a significant average change in y. The estimator, β_1, can be used to construct a test statistic for such a hypothesis test. Thus, one should examine the distribution of estimates, $\hat{\beta}_1$, that would be obtained when samples, each containing n points, are repeatedly drawn from the population of interest, which is the distribution of the multinational-domestic differences in our case. The expected value and variance of S_1 with n periods will be:

$$E(\hat{\beta}_1) = \beta_1,$$

$$\sigma^2_{\beta_1} = \frac{\sigma^2}{\sum\limits_{i=1}^{n} (x_i - \bar{x})^2}$$

Using the relationship above, a z statistic can be constructed:

$$z = \frac{\hat{\beta}_1 - \beta_1}{\sigma_{\beta_1}} = \frac{\hat{\beta}_1 - \beta}{\sigma \Big/ \sqrt{\sum\limits_{i=1}^{n} (x_i - \bar{x})^2}}$$

Since the actual value of σ^2 is unknown, the estimated standard deviation of β_1 should be obtained, which is:

$$s \Big/ \sqrt{\sum\limits_{i=1}^{n} (x_1 - \bar{x})^2}$$

where

$$s = \sqrt{\frac{\sum\limits_{i=1}^{n} (Y_i - Y_i)^2}{n - 2}}$$

Substituting s for σ in z, a test statistics is obtained:

$$t = \frac{B_1}{s} \sqrt{\sum_{i=1}^{n} (x_1 - \bar{x})^2}$$

which can be shown to follow a Student's t distribution in repeated sampling with (n - 2) degrees of freedom. We shall carry out the test with values of $\alpha \leq .20$ (.10 for each tail). If $\alpha = .20$, we have an 80 percent confidence interval. The other values of α are .10, .05, .02, and .01. The lowest α value (highest confidence level) will be taken. Any t value that corresponds to an α value less than .20 will be considered insignificant.

4

The Maturing of
Host Countries

This chapter and the next examine changes in the attitudes of both the host countries and the U.S. multinational corporations during the 1960s and 1970s. There is also a brief look at improvements that have taken place in the field of communications.

The importance of such a study is that once there is an improvement in communications as well as a maturing in the attitudes of both the host countries and the multinationals, then the additional difficulties and risks of operating abroad (over those encountered in operating domestically) will dwindle. Hence the risk premium will fall. This, in turn, ceteris paribus, reduces the cost of equity capital of multinational corporations in relation to that of domestic firms.

A greater emphasis will be placed on the maturing of attitudes in the host country since this is basically an exogenous parameter for the foreign investor. It is also a more controversial topic than the maturing of the multinational firms and improvements in communications.

This chapter does not deal with the benefits to be derived from international diversification. Instead, this is left to a subsequent Chapter in which comparative betas (systematic risks) of the multinational and domestic firms are examined.

By the maturing of the host country is meant the increasing sophistication of the nation state in its relationship vis-a-vis the multinational firm. The attitudes in the 1950s and 1960s were that countries that played host to multinational firms either surrendered unconditionally to such firms and hence allowed them to exploit the country or were very reluctant to allow them inside in the first place. These nations created problems for the multinationals; sometimes the host nations went as far as expropriating and nationalizing their assets. At other times a country is run by a group that finds that it is in its personal interest to allow a foreign company to operate with high profits. Of course, this interest group closely cooperates with the foreign investors and in return is rewarded in various ways. The "banana republics" are typical examples of this type of host country.

On the other hand, in the 1950s and 1960s there was a series of African, Asian, Middle Eastern, and Australasian countries gaining their independence. Since the majority of these countries had undergone a long and unpleasant period of colonial domination by various foreign powers, there had developed an antipathy to industrialized capitalist countries. The new nations viewed with strong suspicion multinational firms, which they thought were acting in connivance with the governments of the countries where their headquarters were based. For instance, they thought that a U.S. multinational would be a tool of the U.S. government.

Thus, the multinational firms were, in general, confronted with two kinds of governments: those that offered them very generous conditions to the point of looking like business partners and those that were highly suspicious of the multinational firms. The latter (which constituted the majority of the developing countries up to the mid-1960s) were very restrictive to the foreign direct investment carried on by multinational firms. The multinationals, in turn, were wary of such countries.

At that time, the multinational firms had not yet matured enough to be able to deal efficiently with such countries. In fact, the developing countries that they were used to dealing with were "banana republics" run by a group whose primary motivation was self-enrichment. Hence, the foreign investor thought that such governments best suited their interest, and the idea that a revolution or a coup d'etat might bring them down was a constant source of worry.

This concern led the investor to require higher profits to compensate for the higher risks that might emanate from a revolution leading to an expropriation. In turn, this raised the anger of those against the "obedient" regime, often to the point of staging a revolution. The risks in the radical and antiforeign investment countries were even higher.

Even in the developed countries (in Europe for example), there was a worry that the U.S. multinational corporations were gradually taking over and supplanting local firms. The very well-known book, Le Defi Americain, by Jean-Jacques Servan-Schreiber openly expressed such worries in the mid-1960s. This book, which was very widely read and eventually became required reading in a large number of business schools in the world, succeeded in spreading the idea that the U.S. multinational firms were on the verge of controlling several European countries, and that there was little that could be done about it. This analysis aroused a wave of reaction against the multinationals in Europe, and various governments began to reexamine their foreign investment regulations.

It is hypothesized in this study that the host governments' attitude toward the multinational firms has been gradually softening during the 1965-78 period, as they have experienced the benefits derived from foreign investment. Rather than seeing the multinational firm in a simplistic black and white perspective, governments began to understand that they had to negotiate intelligently with the prospective investors and that they had to be able to select the kind of investment they needed. This became gradually possible as the developing countries acquired more numerous and more experienced technocrats. So there has been a general move from foreign investment partner governments to national interest governments, on the one hand, and from emotional, economically inexperienced and immature national interest governments to more mature and competent national interest governments on the other hand. As these national interest governments become more competent, they begin to discern the benefits and the costs of foreign investment and strive to obtain the best terms. As Singer and Ansari (1977, p. 212) explain:

> A "development-oriented" government of a developing country has to create an environment in which different economic interest groups co-operate and function in a way that is conducive to the development of the economy. The extent to which the government will be able to influence the different economic groups will depend on its own bargaining strength. . . . A growth in the ability of the LDCs to coordinate the investment policies of the multinationals with their own national development plan will facilitate international economic integration along a pattern that will avoid glaring economic and social imbalances and inequities.

At this stage it is useful to dwell upon the benefits and costs of foreign private direct investment from the host country's point of view in more detail. Starting with the benefits, Gerald Meier (1972, pp. 417-20) mentions the following:

1. It helps to reduce the shortage of domestic savings and increases the supply of foreign exchange.
2. The presence of foreign capital may not only raise the productivity of a given amount of labor, but it may also allow a larger labor force to be employed.
3. If the investment is product innovating, product improving, or cost reducing, consumers may then respectively enjoy new, better-quality, or cheaper products.

4. The government's revenues will be expanded as a result of taxing the foreign investment profits.

5. There may be external economies like the transfer of technological knowledge, market information, managerial and supervisory personnel, organizational experience, and innovations in products and production techniques. It can also stimulate additional domestic investments. For instance, the initial foreign investment can create external investment incentives by raising the demand for the output of other industries.

As for the costs, they are (a) special incentives and concessions offered by the host countries, like tax holidays, financial assistance, subsidies, and the provision of additional public services; (b) adverse effects on domestic savings could arise if foreign investment competes with domestic investment; (c) the return outflow of interest, profit, and dividends on the accumulated investments and repatriation of capital may put pressure on the host country's balance of payments.

After listing the benefits and costs of foreign investment, Reuber (1973, p. 241) and Meier (1972, pp. 420-22) argue that, in general, the benefits clearly outweigh the costs as far as the host country is concerned. This, of course, assumes a minimum of rational economic policy and planning. It is highly probable that this minimum did not exist in the majority of newly independent countries. However, the situation has begun to improve since the mid-1960s.

To show that the attitudes of the host countries toward multinational corporations making direct investments is maturing, two surveys by The Economist will be used, one for Europe and the other for Asian countries, as well as other publications for some of the countries not covered by these surveys. The Economist (1977, p. 5) survey of U.S. companies in Europe indicates that European attitudes toward the U.S. subsidiaries have substantially changed since the mid-1960s. In 1967, Jean-Jacques Servan-Schreiber opened the book that brought him fame, Le Defi Americain, with the following sentence:

Fifteen years from now it is quite possible that the world's third greatest industrial power, just after the United States and Russia, will not be Europe but American industry in Europe.

Servan-Schreiber was more impressed with the U.S. corporations' organizational ability, flexibility, and dynamism as displayed by their fast entries into areas of high technology, growth, and profitability than by their mere weight. Even the dollar weight is not negligible. As mentioned earlier, The Survey of Current Business shows that United States' private direct investment in Western

Europe has increased from $14.0 billion in 1965 to $60.0 billion in 1977, and sales have increased from about $40 billion in 1966 to over $200 billion in 1976. U.S. subsidiaries' sales, which were about 9 percent of the community's GDP in 1966, were over 14 percent in the mid-1970s (The Economist 1977, p. 5). A substantial part of what Servan-Schreiber predicted about the takeover by U.S. firms of European industries has materialized, and yet this does not seem to worry the Europeans as it used to in the mid-1960s (The Economist 1977, p. 5). The Economist (1977, p. 6) describes this situation as "the calm of a sensible people who needed to be woken up, but who have rightly failed to panic at what journalists and academics have told them."

The main reasons for this decrease of European worries are the following:

1. In many sectors, Europe can compete with the United States.

2. Slow as the process may be, the U.S. subsidiaries abroad are acquiring greater influence in U.S. corporate decisions and are not as easily manipulated by the parent company as they used to be.

3. U.S. companies, regardless of how much they remain in U.S. ownership and top management, neither act nor are treated by Washington as instruments of U.S. foreign policy.

4. They have far less freedom of action than what their opponents usually claim. Although they pose problems to Europe's governments, trade unions, and sometimes to local business, they do not escape control. In fact, their liberty seems to be diminishing even further (The Economist 1977, p. 6).

Even when one thinks about the communist parties coming to power in France and Italy, the prospects do not seem to be too bad. The Italian communists say they will welcome continuing multi-national investments. In their common program of 1972, com-munists and socialists have only one foreign company, ITT, on their nationalization list according to The Economist (1977, p. 6) which makes the following statements:

1. All current Western European governments welcome foreign investment.

2. Their employment reasons are stronger than ever and will continue to be so.

3. The local enterprises of multinational companies are seldom thought of as multinational by public opinion (according to a survey carried out by Publicis, a Paris advertising agency).

4. U.S. companies are not known to be from the United States unless they openly claim to be so, like putting the sign "Ford" on the front door.

The following comparative figures give some indication that Europeans had less to fear from United States' direct investment in the mid-1970s than they did in the mid-1960s. In 1964, the world's largest 200 non-U.S. industrial companies sold only 45 percent of what the largest 200 U.S. companies did. In 1976, Fortune's non-U.S. top 500 sold 92 percent as much as the U.S. 500, and among the world's top 50, there were 20 Europeans and only 22 Americans. In 1969 there were seven U.S. banks in the world's largest ten as opposed to three in 1977 (The Economist 1977, p. 6).

To make an a fortiori analysis of the situation, it might be appropriate to look in more detail at the possible rise of Italian communism. By and large, even U.S. managers on the spot have come to terms with it and so have a large number of U.S. headquarters in the east coast, according to a 1974 State Department poll (The Economist 1977, p. 30). Some people even thought that the situation could improve since communist power might bring labor discipline. The only fear was any damage that could happen to the host country's economy as a whole. This worried them more (The Economist 1977, p. 30). The communists have had a milder attitude in recent years toward foreign direct investment than they did in the 1960s. Giorgio Napolitano, a leading communist, said, "We are not opposed to the presence of multinationals, just to some of their behaviour." Another leading communist, Eugenio Peggio, made the following statement: "We do not want to shut them out. . . . or cause them to leave the country . . . we welcome a contribution to the policy of development that we believe is necessary" (The Economist, 1977, p. 30). These statements lead one to believe that the communist view was not one of laissez-faire but as in Canada, one of authorization, for those investments that were thought to be beneficial for the country. The foreigners would bring in the technology, while the state would provide the capital. Nor would the foreign multinational supplant a local firm in an already existing line of production.

These factors indicate that even the communist proposals are not unreasonable. In addition, they guarantee the repatriation of profits and capital. We can see that even the "worst" internal political outcomes in the Western European countries do not look so somber for the U.S. multinationals.

We can now look at another survey of The Economist, which concerns foreign investment in Asia (The Economist 1979). The survey deals with the developing noncommunist countries of Asia. Accordingly these Asian countries, which accounted for 14 percent of the stock of private direct investment of OECD countries in developing countries at the end of 1967, accounted for 26 percent at the end of 1976. In dollar value, the investment, which was $4.9 billion in 1967, role to $19.9 billion in 1976.

These figures indicate that Asian countries have attracted a relatively large amount of foreign investment. Asia has now the largest stock of foreign investment among the developing regions, which comprise South America, Central America, Asia, Africa, the

Middle East, and the developing countries of Europe (The Economist 1979, p. 6). Foreign investors have been attracted by Asia's incentives and reassured by the governments of these countries, which provide an image of safety. The first reason why Asians do not borrow more money rather than taking in foreign investment is that, due to financial risk considerations, equity is preferred to debt. A second and much more important reason is that foreign private direct investment provides not just finance but also technical know-how, all kinds of management skills, jobs, and quite often marketing arrangements (The Economist 1979, pp. 5-6).

Tables 4.1 to 4.11 show which countries were studied in the survey as well as the incentives they offer (The Economist 1979, pp. 8-9). One can observe that in virtually all countries, the investment agencies, most-welcome industries, incentives, ownership requirements, restrictions (if any), royalties, fees, and corporate taxes are explicitly stated. Thus, multinational firms are in a better position to know what to expect.

TABLE 4.1. Asia's Incentives — Hong Kong

Investment agency	Hong Kong Trade Development Council.
Most-welcome industries	Machine tools, precision instruments, foundries, automotive parts.
Special incentives for new investors	Free part. Some concessions on buying and leasing land.
Ownership requirements	No local equity requirements.
Foreign exchange remittance laws	No limits on dividends or capital remittances.
Royalties and fees	No specified limit on remittances. 10 percent of royalties are subject to corporation tax.
Corporate taxation	17 percent on all profits made there. No dividend-withholding tax.

TABLE 4.2. Asia's Incentives — India

Investment agency	Indian Investment Centre.
Most-welcome industries	Fertilizers, insecticides, electrical equipment, scientific instruments, oil machinery.

Special incentives for new investors	Five-year tax holiday on profits up to 7.5 percent of capital employed; grants of up to 15 percent of capital available in backward areas.
Ownership requirements	60 percent Indian equity, except for existing firms with high technology or large exports, where local stake may be 26-49 percent.
Foreign exchange remittance laws	No restrictions on dividend or capital remittances.
Royalties and fees	Usually a maximum of 5 percent of sales value for 5 years.
Corporate taxation	Basic rate 57.5 percent plus 7.5 percent income tax surcharge. Dividend witholding tax is an effective 24.5 percent.

TABLE 4.3. Asia's Incentives – Indonesia

Investment agency	Investment Co-ordinating Board.
Most-welcome industries	Chemicals, pharmaceuticals, medical equipment, raw material processors.
Special incentives for new investors	Priority investors get two- to six-year tax holiday on profits and dividends. Import duties waived.
Ownership requirements	51 percent Indonesian equity for new firms. Those established before 1974 must dilute as they expand.
Foreign exchange remittance level	No restrictions on dividend remittances; capital cannot be repatriated while firm is receiving tax incentives.

| Royalties and fees | Usual maximum of ten years; royalties are tax deductible only up to 2 percent of sales value. |
| Corporate taxation | Minimum rate 20 percent, rising to 45 percent on profits above $25,000. Witholding tax of 20 percent on dividends, royalties, and fees remitted abroad. |

TABLE 4.4. Asia's Incentives – South Korea

Investment agency	Bureau of Foreign Investment Promotion in the Economic Planning Board.
Most-welcome industries	Chemicals, electronics, metal products, food processing, machine tools, pharmaceuticals.
Special incentives for new investors	Five-year tax holiday on all profits, dividends, and royalties; levied at 50 percent of full rates for the next three years.
Ownership requirements	Normally 50 percent local equity required, with exception for high-technology and exporting firms.
Foreign exchange remittance laws	No dividend restrictions; up to 20 percent of capital may be remitted each year after two years of operation.
Royalties and fees	Normally up to 3 percent of sales, though flat fees are increasingly common – up to $100,000 automatically.
Corporate taxation	20 percent basic rate, higher bands up to 40 percent. Dividend-witholding tax up to 25 percent. Publicly quoted

companies pay lower rates
than closed companies.

TABLE 4.5. Asia's Incentives – Malaysia

Investment agency	Federal Industrial Development Authority.
Most-welcome industries	Chemicals, wood products, food processing, animal feedstuffs, most rubber products, electrical appliances, electronics, precision instruments.
Special incentives for new investors	Priority sectors get two- to ten-year tax holidays, depending on location, technology, and export performance.
Ownership requirements	Aim is to have 70 percent Malaysian ownership by 1990 (30 percent Malay, 40 percent other Malaysian). Exceptions for high-technology and exporting firms.
Foreign exchange remittance laws	No restrictions on dividend or capital remittances.
Royalties and fees	Usually 2-3 percent of sales for 5 years.
Corporate taxation	Basic rate 40 percent, plus 5 percent development and, for some, 5 percent excess profits tax. No witholding tax on dividends.

TABLE 4.6. Asia's Incentives – Pakistan

Investment agency	Investment Promotion Bureau.
Most-welcome industries	Chemicals, steel mills, shipbuilding, electronics, jute products, fertilizers, petrochemicals, engineering.
Special incentives for new investors	Five-year tax holiday for firms setting up in

	depressed regions; others receive tax credits. Special rebates on exports.
Ownership requirements	No legal requirements, but joint ventures are favored – 51 percent local participation.
Foreign exchange remittance laws	No restrictions on dividend or capital remittances.
Royalties and fees	Generally 3 percent of sales for 5 years, although favored products may be allowed up to 5 percent of sales.
Corporate taxation	Foreign companies usually subject to 50 percent profits tax. 15 percent dividend-witholding tax.

TABLE 4.7. Asia's Incentives – Philippines

Investment agency	Board of investments.
Most-welcome industries	Chemicals, steel mills, ship-building, electronics, farm products, wood products.
Special incentives for new investors	Accelerated depreciation allowances, and partial tax holidays for up to ten years.
Ownership requirements	60-70 percent local equity required for most projects; favored new entrants can start at 100 percent but must dilute within 40 years.
Foreign exchange remittance laws	No restrictions on dividend remittances or capital for investments made since March 1973.
Royalties and fees	Up to 5 percent of sales for up to 5 years with very few exceptions.
Corporate taxation	Basic rate of 25 percent, higher band of 35 percent, with extra tax of 5 percent if rate

of return on capital ex-
ceeds 10 percent. 10
percent dividend-with-
holding tax.

TABLE 4.8. Asia's Incentives – Singapore

Investment agency	Economic Development Board.
Most-welcome industries	Chemicals, aircraft compo- nents, scientific in- struments, machine tools.
Special incentives for new investors	Tax holiday of five to ten years, accelerated de- preciation, cheap government loans.
Ownership requirements	No local equity require- ments.
Foreign exchange remittance laws	No restrictions on dividend or capital remittances.
Royalties and fees	No limits.
Corporate taxation	40 percent profit tax. No dividend-witholding tax, but tax on royal- ties and fees of 20-40 percent.

TABLE 4.9. Asia's Incentives – Sri Lanka

Investment agency	Greater Colombo Economic Commission.
Most-welcome industries	Electronics, food pro- cessing, pharmaceuticals, leather, rubber and wood products, light engineering.
Special incentives for new investors	Five- to ten-year tax holiday, then exporters pay 2 percent tax on their sales and 10 percent tax on royalty payments.
Ownership requirements	No legal requirements.
Foreign exchange remittance laws	No restrictions on dividend or capital remittances.
Royalties and fees	15-30 percent royalty tax after tax holiday ends.

Corporate taxation	50 percent profits tax plus 5 percent for foreign companies. Dividend-witholding tax of 33 percent.

TABLE 4.10. Asia's Incentives – Taiwan

Investment agency	Industrial Development and Investment Centre.
Most-welcome industries	Chemicals, electrical machinery, cameras, transport equipment, machine tools.
Special incentives for new investors	Five-year tax holiday (excluding dividend-withholding tax) or accelerated deprecia-tion.
Ownership requirements	No legal requirements but joint ventures favored.
Foreign exchange remittance laws	No restrictions on dividend remittances; 15 percent of capital may be remitted each year after two years of operation.
Royalties and fees	Generally 3-5 percent of sales.
Corporate taxation	Basic rate of 25 percent, higher band of 35 percent. Dividend-withholding tax of 20 percent. Royalties and fees sent abroad are subject to 20 percent tax.

TABLE 4.11. Asia's Incentives – Thailand

Investment agency	Board of Investment.
Most-welcome industries	Chemicals, electrical machinery, car compo-nents, metal processing, pulp and paper, food processing.

Special incentives for new investors	Three- to eight-year tax holiday plus further tax concessions for companies locating in depressed regions.
Ownership requirements	51 percent local ownership; exceptions made for priority industries.
Foreign exchange remittance laws	No restrictions on dividend remittances; 20 percent of capital may be remitted each year after two years of operation.
Royalties and fees	Agreements scrutinized; wide range of terms allowed.
Corporate taxation	30 percent rate for publicly quoted companies, 35 percent for others. 25 percent dividend-withholding tax, and royalties sent abroad.

Although Asian governments set up or are partners in business enterprises, nationalizations have become nil at present. South Korea, Singapore, and Taiwan have never nationalized any foreign companies. Among the other countries, Pakistan was the last to nationalize business, and that was in the early and mid-1970s. It was directed against local magnates (the famous "twenty-two families"), and foreign investment was hardly touched at all (The Economist 1979, p. 23). Another example would be the Philippines, which used to be the most restrictive country as far as the repatriation of royalties was concerned. Before 1974, it allowed only 50 percent of the royalties to be repatriated. Today, they can all be remitted, but only for five years (which might be extended) and up to 5 percent of the wholesale output value, which is generous in relation to what is generally accorded in the world (The Economist 1979, p. 23). So, it can be deduced that the investment climate has become less risky than before for multinationals.

The following countries or groups of countries, which have not been treated in the two surveys above, have been examined by Price Waterhouse Information Guide for Doing Business in. . . reports.

We have tried our best within the constraint of available reports to compare different spots in time, for instance 1967 and 1977, to see if any changes in the host countries' attitudes toward foreign investment has taken place. These Price Waterhouse guides or reports neither treat all countries in the world nor do they go back to the 1960s for each country they study. Yet, the following survey of these reports still gives some substantial indications of changes in attitudes. The last two countries, Syria and Turkey, have been examined from sources other than the Price Waterhouse guides. For the other countries, the dates and pages at the end of the following sections indicate the dates and pages of the respective Price Waterhouse guides.

Chile. Chile, Colombia, Peru, Bolivia, Ecuador, and Venezuela have ratified Decision 24 of the Andean Pact, which deals with the treatment of foreign capital and trademarks, patents, licenses, and royalties. This has brought a few restrictions on new foreign investment. However, the specific rules are determined by each country individually.

Except for the Allende interlude, there has been a generally favorable attitude toward foreign investment in Chile, and the rules have been made more explicit by Decree Law No. 600 of July 13, 1974 which, in some instances, is even more attractive than the rules that existed before. (See Price Waterhouse (September 1969; January 1975, pp. 8-9.)

Colombia. A comparison of the 1971 and 1978 guides indicates that the favorable attitude of the Colombian government toward foreign investment is continuing. (See Price Waterhouse January 1971, p. 4; April 1978, p. 13.)

Venezuela. Until 1974, there were few restrictions on foreign investment. The entry by Venezuela into the Andean Pact will somewhat increase the restrictions and controls on new investors and even existing investors. In addition Venezuela has brought Decrees 62 and 63 of its own, which also restrict foreign investment. Hence, in the Venezuelan case, we see a hardening line toward foreign investment. (See Price Waterhouse April 1969; February 1975, pp. 4-10.)

Argentina. A study of the 1970 and 1975 guides indicates that no fundamental changes occurred as far as the attitudes of Argentina toward foreign direct investors, except that the conditions, prohibitions, priorities, preferences, transfer and reinvestment of profits, repatriation of capital, restrictions, etc., are more clearly enunciated. (See Price Waterhouse September 1970; February 1975, pp. 5-13.)

Central America. The official attitude of the respective governments has been friendly toward private foreign investment. Only minor restrictions are encountered by foreign investors, who are accorded the same rights and privileges as nationals. In accordance with the Central American Economic Integration Agreement, Costa Rica, El Salvador, Guatemala, Honduras, and Nicaragua have agreed to equalize their industrial development laws.

In order to encourage the transfer of U.S. private capital and technology to developing countries, the U.S. government, through the Overseas Private Investment Corporation, will, under certain circumstances, guarantee a firm against political and business risks. (See Price Waterhouse February 1969; December 1976, p. 12.)

Mexico. The Price Waterhouse guide of 1972 (p. 12) states that "the Echeverria administration has announced its intention of maintaining approximately the same attitude as its predecessor, with perhaps somewhat more positive attempts to obtain new investment, foreign as well as local, in specific areas of the economy." The Law for the Promotion of Mexican Investment and Regulation of Foreign Investment of March 9, 1973 codified many of the rules by the December 14, 1973 law (No. 20557) on foreign investment. This explicitness is likely to reduce uncertainty for foreign investors as this host country's demands and expectations become more predictable. (See Price Waterhouse February 1972; August 1977, pp. 18-20.)

Brazil. The relatively mild attitude of the Brazilian government toward foreign investment has become even more encouraging by allowing investments in the Brazilian stock market by the Decree-Law No. 1401 dated May 7, 1975. (See Price Waterhouse June 1970; June 1975, Supplement, pp. 11-20.)

Uruguay. The Price Waterhouse guide of 1973 states that a number of laws that grant privileges and concessions with respect to a variety of taxes, including import and export taxes, have been enacted to attract foreign capital. In addition, exemption from income taxes is granted to "new industries" for a period of ten years and permanently to income arising from the export of locally manufactured goods in the proportion that such exports bear to total sales. In addition, protection against competitive foreign imports may be obtained under certain conditions regarding foreign investment that were already being applied as administrative policies. It also has brought a few new limitations on new investments but was not intended to be retroactive as far as the maximum percentage (49 percent) of foreign control is concerned. There are no restrictions on the repatriation of funds. (See Price Waterhouse July 1970; April 1973, p. 7.)

Canada. Twenty years ago there were virtually no restrictions on foreign ownership in Canada. Today, however, foreign investors who wish to acquire control of an existing Canadian business must demonstrate to a Canadian Foreign Investment Review Agency that their proposed investment will be a significant benefit to Canada. It should be stressed such a change will reduce possible friction rather than increase it, since foreign companies (mainly from the United States) that have passed these tests are not likely to be very much harrassed after that. Canada is the country with the largest stock of foreign investment in the world and owes a great deal of its high standard of living to foreign investment. As the Price Waterhouse guide mentions, "It is not the intention of the Canadian Government to block all foreign direct investment in Canada but to ensure that such investment will be in the best interest of Canadians." (See Price Waterhouse, 1975, p. 9.)

Australia. The Australian government accepts that foreign capital has in the past played a vital role in Australia's economic growth and that significant benefits would flow from future new investment from overseas. However, while encouraging overseas capital, the government now seeks to ensure that new foreign investment is on an equitable basis, which shares the net benefits between the foreign investor and the Australian community. In brief, the government intends to make in advance a cost-benefit study of the new investment. This, we believe, is likely to decrease possible points of friction that could eventually arise. (See Price Waterhouse February 1970; June 1978, pp. 12-13.)

South Africa. It is the South African government's policy to offer encouragement to foreign companies wishing to establish sub-sidiaries or branches in South Africa. The high level of foreign investment has had a positive effect on economic development. In addition, the government decided to supply services or equipment to investors willing to go into sectors of high priority in the 1974-79 Economic Development Plan. (See Price Waterhouse February 1967; August 1977, pp. 17-18.)

Kuwait. With the aim of speeding up growth in sectors other than oil, Kuwait has adopted the policy of encouraging foreign invest-ment to attract the most highly developed technology and greatest expertise in these sectors. Foreign investors may import their raw material free of duties, whereas there will be high duties for those imported products that have local counterparts. (See Price Water-house April 1975, pp. 9-12.)

Saudi Arabia. In 1964, a Foreign Capital Investment Code was introduced in Saudi Arabia to assist foreign investors. Under this code, foreign investment is encouraged for economic development projects outside the petroleum sector and where projects are approved by the Foreign Investment Capital Committee. The same favorable climate for foreign investment continues today. (See Price Waterhouse October 1975, p. 11.)

United Arab Emirates. Ever since the U.A.E. rulers have begun to consider economic development more systematically, foreign investment of capital know-how and personnel has been welcome in the U.A.E. provided it is to their benefit. In the late 1960s, the individual emirates granted special incentives like tax holidays, free land, capital, and elimination of import duties. (See Price Waterhouse January 1976, pp. 11, 14-15.)

Bahrain. The main incentives in Bahrain are the absence of taxes, the availability of skilled local labor, cheap fuel, relatively easy transport and communications, and repatriation without restriction of capital, profits, and earnings of any sort. (See Price Waterhouse November 1977, p. 12.)

Morocco. The Moroccan government generally welcomes foreign investment as can be attested by the Investment Code of 1973, which was designed to stimulate such investments. The opportunities for foreigners to invest in Morocco are particularly good in sectors where the foreign investor can contribute to the transfer of technology and to employment. (See Price Waterhouse May 1977, p. 8.)

Iran. The Iranian government during the Shah's regime was favorably inclined to foreign investment, especially in sectors where there was insufficient local expertise. In 1979, the Shah's regime collapsed and was replaced by an Islamic Republic which, even though not against foreign investment per se, is against what it terms the extravagance and erroneous policy of the former regime. Although no clear policy has yet been enunciated on foreign investment, the majority of foreign firms have shut doors in Iran and follow a wait-and-see policy until the government's attitude crystallizes. For the time being, we can say that the climate for foreign investors has deteriorated in Iran. (See Price Waterhouse October 1975, p. 10.)

Syria. An interesting case is that of Syria, a country with a Baathist socialist regime, which was known to have a hardline attitude toward foreign investment. After 1976, Syria became more willing than it was before to countenance wide-ranging attractions for foreign investors (Sakr 1977, p. 66). Accordingly, Syria offers them tax exemptions for three to seven years and, in certain sectors, the right to import construction material and furniture free of duty. In addition, foreign investors are allowed to withdraw capital and profits in any currency, subject only to existing Central Bank regulations (Sakr 1977, p. 67).

Turkey. A 1976 official report of the State Planning Organization proposes that Turkey should actively invite foreign corporations that want to invest in sectors or projects deemed beneficial by Turkey, rather than passively wait for foreign investors to come by themselves (Oguz 1976, p. 164). The main reasons for the increased interests of Turkey in foreign investment are financing needs as well as the transfer of advanced technology.

Ajami (1979), who makes a survey of Arab countries' response to the rapidly increasing operations of multinational corporations in the Middle East reaches conclusions that seem to be reassuring for the multinationals. Ajami sets out to examine the attitudes of decision makers – the educated Arab elite – toward multinational corporations. Ajami's detailed questionnaire covers nationalism, the transfer of technology, and economic ideology. The survey includes two countries with contrasting political views: Kuwait and Iraq. Considering the differences between these two societies, the results of the survey show a surprising uniformity. For instance, 82 percent of both Iraqis and Kuwaitis agreed that multinationals contributed to economic growth, development, industrialization, and local skill formation, while 72 percent thought that the net contribution of multinationals was positive, regardless of the costs. Ajami concludes that host-country elites appeal to the local public opinion with radical rhetoric while following more moderate and rational relations with the multinational corporations that they publicly criticize. As we shall see a little further on, Frank (1980) reached similar conclusions on a worldwide survey.

The vast majority of the United States' private foreign direct investments lies in the countries examined above, although the list was not exhaustive. It would, therefore, not be erroneous to draw conclusions from such a set. We have seen that, except for a few, these countries have made the foreign investment climate more attractive and/or more explicit. Both of these factors are encouraging foreign investment. Hence, these factors will lead to a reduction of uncertainty and, we hypothesize, should contribute to reducing the cost of capital or risk.

According to Frank (1980, p. 10), private flows from industrial to developing countries have grown in significance (see Table 4.12).

In a recent and comprehensive study, Frank (1980) indicates that an important evolution has taken place in the attitudes of many developing countries and transnational corporations. The countries' earlier fears of the power of the transnationals have been decreasing, and they look at the companies from a more pragmatic and less ideological perspective. At the same time, the multinationals show a greater concern for the developing countries and are more willing to adapt their policies and operations to the realities of changing national goals in these countries. This second trend will be treated in the next chapter.

According to Frank, much of the early tension between host countries and multinational corporations after World War II arose from an understandable determination on the part of many LDCs to

TABLE 4.12. Net Flow[a] of Financial Resources to Developing Countries from Industrial Countries[b] – 1960-78 (in millions of dollars)

	Average 1960-65	Average 1966-71	1972	1973	1974	1975	1976	1977	1978
Official development assistance	5,494	6,663	8,538	9,378	11,317	13,585	13,734	14,696	18,308
Other official flows	379	773	1,546	2,463	2,183	3,024	3,296	3,319	(4,000)[c]
Private flows	3,186	6,020	8,333	9,458	7,330	22,152	20,872	29,988	(32,820)
Direct investment	1,789	2,902	4,234	4,719	1,124	10,494	7,824	8,792	(9,470)
Bilateral portfolio	536	818	1,984	3,286	3,795	5,313	5,166	10,454	(11,350)
Multilateral portfolio	201	513	667	257	-70	2,278	3,059	2,642	(2,000)
Export credits	660	1,794	1,448	1,196	2,481	4,067	4,823	8,100	(10,000)
Grants by private voluntary agencies	NA[d]	NA	1,036	1,364	1,217	1,342	1,357	1,489	(1,500)
Total net flow[e]	9,059	13,456	19,453	22,663	22,047	40,103	39,260	49,492	(56,628)

[a]Gross disbursements less amortization receipts on earlier lending. The figure includes flows to multilateral organizations.

[b]The countries include Australia, Austria, Belgium, Canada, Denmark, France, Germany, Italy, Japan, the Netherlands, New Zealand, Norway, Sweden, Switzerland, the United Kingdom, and the United States. Also included is the Commission of the European Economic Community.

[c]Parentheses denote estimates.

[d]NA = not available.

[e]Figures prior to 1972 exclude New Zealand.

Sources: Organization for Economic Cooperation and Development, Development Assistance, 1961-71 issues; Organization for Economic Cooperation and Development, Development Cooperation, 1972-78 issues. Figures for 1978 are from OECD Press Release, June 19, 1979. Figures slightly modified to reflect World Bank data.

consolidate political and economic control after long periods of foreign domination. The resulting governmental intervention was viewed negatively by multinational corporations. By the late 1960s, however, it became increasingly clear to the multinationals that the gist of the problem had little to do with ideology. The fact that very profitable and stable arrangements were concluded with the socialist countries of Eastern Europe is meaningful. These include joint ventures and technology sales agreements. With stronger governments and a clearer sense of national purpose, the LDCs have generally been able to offer the multinational firms more solid and well-defined conditions (Frank 1980, pp. 25-26).

Frank (1980, pp. 25-26) contends that, with few exceptions, multinational firms presently emphasize instability, not ideology, as the main hurdle to investing and operating overseas. Penrose (1971, p. 237) also writes that multinationals tend to invest where they think it is profitable regardless of ideological considerations in the host country. A comprehensive empirical study for developing countries by Levis (1979) seems to support Penrose's view. Levis finds that multinationals attach more importance to economic considerations than to political ones when investing in developing countries. Frank (1980, pp. 25-26) mentions that instability does not necessarily mean political upheavals followed by changes in regime. Such conditions may curtail foreign investment temporarily but as the new regime consolidates its position, foreign investment will recover. Far more consequential are those forms of instability that need not result from internal political upheavals. These are threats of political action, changes in conditions of operation such as ownership and remittance regulations, complex and drawn-out bureaucratic procedures, and more generally, the prospect of arbitrary and unpredictable alterations in the rules of the game after investment decisions have been made. Naturally, the foreign investor cannot expect a foreign environment that is totally free of such instability and arbitariness. However, there is a certain level that is tolerable.

Major factors that hamper stability in most LDCs are mass poverty and explosive population growth. According to Frank (1980, pp. 27-29), there are five forces of a more general and fundamental nature that lead to instability and tension between the LDCs and the multinational firms.

Rapid Growth and Increased Bargaining Power. Rapid growth normally gives increased bargaining power to developing countries. Rapid growth means increasing gross national product. In turn, this means an increasing internal market that may cross the threshold for an even more quickly expanding internal market for the type of discretionary products that many multinationals specialize in. Moreover, a sustained increase of per capita GNP often facilitates better education and technical skills, a more advanced infrastructure, as well as institutions that attract multinationals, which then invest not only for the local market but also for exports from the host country. However, these developments will also alter the conditions under which the original agreement between the host country and the multinational corporation took place. The conditions of regulation and control applicable to foreign enterprise change, thus undermining the basis for incentives and priorities accorded to it.

Altered National Goals. As the socioeconomic structure of a country changes, its national goals may be altered concomitantly. For instance, at an early stage of development, a country may be contented to have multinationals working for import substitution. After a certain time, however, the host country may feel that this is insufficient and may demand export-oriented production as well. As the domestic market becomes saturated with domestic goods and the limits of import substitution become apparent, a country may shift to a policy of export promotion involving a devaluation of its currency, a possible reduction of protective tariffs, and other penalties and rewards to encourage exports. In addition, the host country may ask the foreign investors to help facilitate a more equitable distribution of income and the reduction of unemployment. Such shifting priorities create an atmosphere of uncertainty for the multinational corporations.

The Obsolescent Bargain. The obsolescent bargain is especially apt to take place in the case of natural resources where the host country may have a greater degree of leverage. Factors such as the volume of production, control of the operations, pricing of the product, and the division of the profits may lead to a renegotiation of the original deal. A striking but not unique example may be seen in the developments that took place in countries that are members of the Organization of Petroleum Exporting Countries (OPEC) after 1973.

Scapegoating. Multinational corporations have often been used as scapegoats in both developed and developing countries when governments face difficult straits while trying to satisfy the needs and aspirations of their people. They may be blamed for stifling local entrepreneurs, meddling in local politics, being tools of the home country (especially the United States), and destroying the indigenous culture. They may also be accused of trying to make profits at the expense of public welfare. These accusations, whether they are real, imagined, or exaggerated, are apt to be used to divert the attention of public opinion away from the problems faced by the government.

Succession of Dilemmas. At a certain stage of development, a country may want advanced technology that is capital intensive. At another stage, it may want less-advanced and more labor-intensive technology, which could alleviate rising unemployment. At times, the repatriation of profits by the multinational may look bad. At other times, the reinvestment of these profits in the local economy may look undesirable because it may convey the feeling to some people that it wants to increase its control over the host country. As they attempt to resolve dilemmas such as the above, developing countries are shifting their policies in response to their changing perceptions of how to maximize their gains from the foreign investment process.

After stating the above forces, Frank continued his study, which is based on detailed interviews with top management from 90 multinational corporations based in the United States, Japan, Australia, the United Kingdom, Germany, France, Sweden, and other European countries. The results of these interviews show that the five forces mentioned above are indeed those thought to have top priority by higher management. Thus, clear and well-defined goals, which have less chances of eventually changing, are very important factors for foreign investors. According to Frank (1980, pp. 40-42), the majority of multinational corporations gave Asian countries, particularly Malaysia and India, high marks for the clarity with which they express their general development objectives. Except for Nigeria, African nations were also seen in that light. However, the top managers held a generally dimmer view of Latin American and Caribbean countries. Still, Brazil and Colombia were cited as having clear and well-defined goals, while Peru and Mexico were thought to have more ambiguous goals. Multinationals mentioned that, just as in developed countries, it was possible to see goals that were contradictory in developing countries. For instance, a host country may require that corporations build small-scale labor-intensive facilities and may then ask them to export, despite the generally higher costs of this mode of production. Sometimes, the utopian goals set by developing countries may be impossible to carry out due to administrative, legal, financial, cultural, and tech-nological constraints. Moreover, two neighboring countries that started with import-substitution-oriented foreign investment may both end up simultaneously requiring the multinationals to export into each other's market. Despite these inconsistencies, most multi-nationals felt that developing countries made their goals clearer. Also, despite their flamboyant antimultinational corporation public declarations, the host-country technocrats become far more reasonable in private negotiations. Multinational firm managers asserted that developing country technocrats realized both the benefits of foreign investment and the total disregard of local firms toward national goals. Multinationals producing consumption goods that are not indispensable for the economy try even harder to conform to national goals since they have less bargaining power. Few multinationals thought that these conflicts are fundamental or irreconcilable. They mentioned that the disagreements are usually on matters of detail and degree and are less important than the underlying common interest. Hence, they generally suggested that differences could be resolved through negotiation and compromise. Most multinationals stated that they would like host countries to define their national goals clearly in a legal and regulatory framework. Thus there would be fewer chances of potential conflict.

When Frank (1980, pp. 111-12) asked multinational executives about deterrents to investment, they generally said that deterrents to investment in the developing countries are matters of degree, not absolutes. For instance, a policy like export requirements may be acceptable when pursued in moderation. However, if it is pushed to extreme, it may make it intolerable for the foreign investor. Naturally the level of tolerance will change according to the bargaining power of a firm. Resource firms do not have much leverage since they have to go where the minerals are. Firms found that the instability and the resultant uncertainty are the most important deterrents. Instability is seen in two forms. First, it arises from the sudden and frequent changes in government or in government policy dealing with major changes in the rules of the game, which affects both parties. Secondly, a lack of clarity in goals causes day-to-day arbitrariness and inconsistencies of interpretation of laws and regulations. However, the managers said these two sorts of instability were to be found in both developed and developing countries. They stated that if the terms of operation are clear and stable, they can invest anywhere regardless of the stringency of the regulations as long as there is some margin for profit. Subsidiaries in Eastern Europe were mentioned as an example to this kind of consideration. This does not mean that host-country regulations and ideology do not matter at all. However multinational managers saw them as much less important than instability and unpredictability, which they felt were decreasing.

Frank (1980, p. 146) states that longer contact and experience with multinationals has given host-country governments a better understanding of how the multinational firms operate and an appreciation that the relationship need not be of a zero-sum kind, but one which can be beneficial to both parties. In many developing countries, stronger economies as well as better trained individuals have led to greater competence and rationality vis-a-vis the multinational corporations. This, of course, is conducive to a more pragmatic outlook.

5

The Maturing of Multinational Firms and Improvement of Communications

THE MATURING OF MULTINATIONAL FIRMS

Corporations and business enterprises in general are in a continuous process of evolution, modernization, and sophistication. This is true from both the technical, organizational, and managerial points of view. More and more people of higher caliber are joining the ranks of entrepreneurs, business executives, and experts. For instance, a study of the educational level of entrepreneurs by Douglass (1976, p. 41) indicates that college graduate entrepreneurs, who were only 6 percent of the total in 1961, rose to 28 percent in 1975. This was a much faster increase in comparison to the educational process of the U.S. population in general. A study by Weller (1973, pp. 25-26, 36) shows that the number of Ph.Ds and D.B.As entering the ranks of business executives, advisors, and consultants is rapidly growing. Hence, it would not be farfetched to state that managerial competence in business firms is on the increase. This should be especially true of the multinational firms, which are usually large corporations with ample resources, which enable them to acquire top talent. For instance, in the mid-1960s, quantitative political risk analysts were a rarity even among very large multinationals. It was a novelty even among academics. However, by the late 1960s and early 1970s, the academic research on the topic considerably increased, and after the mid-1970s, most multinational firms began to employ quantitative political risk analysts or teams of them.

In addition to the improvement of the educational background of the line and staff members of the firm, the multinationals have become more experienced in dealing with the nation states since the 1950s and 1960s. Their attitudes toward international business have changed. Before, the multinationals were thinking of making high profits in a short span of time, especially in developing countries. Now, they are more inclined to think of operating abroad on a more long-term basis and to take the goals and requirements of the host countries much more into account than before. They also hire many more local staff than before.

In 1950, Hans Singer suggested that "a flow of international investment into the under-developed countries will contribute to their economic development only if it is absorbed into their economic system; i.e., if a good deal of complementary domestic investment is generated and the requisite domestic resources are found". This, of course, is also true of the contribution of international investment to the economic growth of developed industrial countries. U.S. multinational firms in the late 1950s and throughout the 1960s began to realize the importance of this idea and acted accordingly. During that period, the contribution of U.S. investors to economic growth is what has lead many developed and developing countries to encourage foreign investment (Wilkins 1974, p. 400).

An interesting finding of Frank (1980, pp. 144-46) is that there is a basic sympathy among the multinationals for the general goals of the developing host countries. The managers do not question the legitimacy of host countries' evaluating the costs and benefits of foreign investment in the light of the countries' goals. An important evolution has taken place in the attitudes of multinationals toward the growth process in the developing countries and toward their relationship with that process. To a much greater extent than in the 1950s and 1960s, the multinationals recognize both the diversity of circumstances in the developing world and their own need for flexibility vis-a-vis individual developing countries. They also realize that history need not be repetitive. Thus, the developing countries of today do not necessarily have to follow the same path as the Europeans did during the eighteenth and nineteenth centuries. Many Third World countries are facing dilemmas of population explosion and poverty, which were never faced by the Western countries during their initial industrializations.

This kind of understanding has led a major part of the multinationals to show a greater willingness to accept the constraints set by the developing countries. They also realize that these constraints are often beneficial in the long run since they reduce possibilities of future frictions. Of course, this kind of a maturing of the multinationals may also be due to increasing competition, which makes them more compromising. Frank (1980, p. 145) gives examples of such accommodations. Most multinationals employ and train host-country nationals for their foreign operations not only for unskilled and skilled manual jobs but also for technical and managerial positions. The managing director of the local subsidiary is often a local national. Multinationals, which were formerly reluctant to accept joint ventures, are far more prone to do so now.

The reorganization of foreign activities by multinationals is another evolution that is worth examining. The reorganization is oriented toward the multinationalization of management and of capital. This evolution, which has been taking place since the 1950s and 1960s, is continuing. The essential purpose of reorganizing a multinational firm is to try to optimize the degree of integration of elements spread geographically. According to Widing (1973, pp. 153-60) and Phatak (1971, p. 109), multinationals made more frequent reorganizations of their activities in the 1970s. Naturally, there are advantages and disadvantages both for centralization and decentralization. Thus, the multinational firm should attempt to find an equilibrium point. Widing (1973, p. 157) thinks the U.S. firms, which tended to underestimate national and geographical differences in the 1950s and 1960s, were overestimating them in the 1970s.

Widing (1973) writes that multinational corporations should be geographically decentralized to be able to react rapidly to frequent changes in the local market. A decentralized organization can be according to geographical areas, to product lines, or to functions, depending on the circumstances. On the other hand, in order to have a general strategy and economies of scale, international activities must be well integrated to the entire corporation. Most of the firms that have been examined have been trying to take both factors into account by superimposing an international division on a multiproduct and multidivision structure in the parent country. Widing observes that domestic and foreign operations have little integration during the first stages of their growth but become more integrated in ulterior stages. Lorange (1976) makes similar observations. Thus, such an evolution in the organizations of multinationals should lead to improved performance and reduced risk. Sadchev (1977, pp. 33-39) and Salama (1978, pp. 259-98) write that the multinationalization of management and capital, which means more non-U.S. managers and more joint ventures, has rendered multinationals less prone to conflicts with the host countries, besides improving their performance. Alpander (1973) mentions that locally recruited managers understand the local environment better than their expatriate U.S. counterparts.

One must also mention the international advisory board, which is another development that tends to reduce risk. Hill (1976, pp. 28-31) writes that the board consists of U.S. and non-U.S. business authorities, who are very knowledgeable of economic, political, and social problems in their countries. The role of the board, which meets on a regular basis, is to inform the parent company about the latest developments. The international advisory boards could be considered as a first step toward the multinationalization of higher management. This, of course, should contribute to decentralization.

Exchange risks play a very important role in the decision about how much to centralize. In multinational corporations, there are real financial flows among the subsidiaries as well as between the parent company and the subsidiaries. The parent company could supply the subsidiary with goods for which there is to be a payment and vice versa. Also, there are reciprocal short- and long-term agreements that necessitate the payment of interests. The multinational corporation can protect itself against exchange risks by means of a variety of methods that require some centralization.

The leads-and-lags method consists of delaying debts in weak currencies as much as possible while paying debts in strong currencies as soon as possible. For instance, if the U.S. dollar is expected to undergo a devaluation, U.S. importers could accelerate their payments in the stronger German mark and thus avoid losses. German importers, on the other hand, will want to wait until after the devaluation, which will mean a smaller payment in marks but the same payment in dollars.

The excess liquidities of the parent company and/or the subsidiaries could be collected in a pool located outside the home country. The parent company and/or the subsidiaries that need funds could borrow from this pool and thus avoid borrowing from banks. This is another method of financing that reduces exchange risks.

Another method of reducing exchange risks is to borrow money in countries that have weak currencies or low interest rates and then lend the funds to subsidiaries in countries with strong currencies or high interest rates.

There is a very widespread use of transfer prices among the multinationals. The different fiscal systems in different countries lead the multinationals to manipulate transfer prices in such a way that profits look highest in the country with the lowest tax rate. Hanson (1975, pp. 857-65) gives examples of this technique.

All the above techniques require a degree of centralization. However, as we mentioned before, overcentralization can also be harmful. So the multinational corporations need to find an optimal degree of coordination. As their experience increases, they would naturally reduce their risks by getting closer to this optimum.

It can thus be said that the multinational firm not only has increased the competence of its personnel but also has gained considerable experience in international operations. These factors and the maturing of the host countries, as explained before, have led the multinational firm to think in a longer time perspective and hence to take the needs of the host countries more into account. Such an attitude should lead to a greater understanding between the multinationals and the host countries, and thus the possibility of friction will be reduced. This, of course, should reduce the risks of operating abroad, leading to a lower cost of equity capital.

THE IMPROVEMENT OF COMMUNICATIONS

The exchange of information between home-office and subsidiary management is an important factor in coordinating and controlling multinational operations. Communications between home-office and subsidiary management can be classified into two categories: personal exchanges such as visits, meetings, and telephone conversations, and impersonal communications such as regular reports, budgets, plans, telexes, and letters (Brandt and Hulbert 1976, p. 57). U.S. multinationals communicate with their subsidiaries more heavily than European multinationals do. U.S. multinationals are far more inclined to hold regular management meetings on a regional or worldwide basis (Brandt and Hulbert 1976, p. 57).

It is well known that communications have vastly and rapidly improved not only during the last two centuries, but especially during the last two decades. It would be appropriate to quote Clapham (1975, pp. 9-10) about the development of communications that facilitated the growth of multinational enterprise.

In 1934 a man who needed to make personal contact with subsidiary companies in, say, India, Malaya, and Australia would have been absent from his desk for three or four months; in 1974 you feel self-indulgent if you allow three weeks for the job. Correspondence round the world still takes three or four days, but you can dial a number in San Francisco or Stockholm in a minute; and all the time your computers chat away intercontinentally. . . . multinational working is no longer adventurous or laborious: it is merely normal.

The developments that took place since the 1950s and early 1960s are quite substantial. Telephone communications were relatively time consuming because of the waiting time involved, and audibility was poor. At present, there is not even the need to call the operator, since direct international dialing has become possible. Moreover, audibility has greatly improved. The telex has become very widespread, and its technology has improved.

In addition, world flights have increased in number and speed. For instance, the Concorde covers the distance between Europe and the United States in about three and a half hours. This would enable more frequent meetings of high-level executives whose time is scarce.

Examples could be multiplied, and we do not want to dwell on the obvious. One can conclude that, because of improved communications, the multinational corporation's knowledge of what happens in the subsidiaries and in the world in general has increased in speed, quality, and volume. This situation should tend to reduce uncertainty and hence risk and the cost of equity capital.

6

Test Results

This chapter contains the results of the empirical tests, which use four different methods. The first method deals with the cost of equity capital (k_e) using forward-looking growth during the period 1965-78 (see Figures 6.1-6.18). Here, the graphs of actual data as well as the linear trends are shown for the average of all groups as well as for each industrial group.

The second method looks at the cost of equity capital (k_e) with historical growth during the period 1965-78 (see Figures 6.19-6.23). Our main purpose for using this method is to compare k_e using historical growth with forward-looking growth. Thus, only the overall average has been taken into account. As explained in Chapter 3, our essential cost of equity capital calculation method is the one that uses forward-looking rates. For the overall averages of both methods, we have drawn linear least-square trend lines for the periods 1965-78, 1965-70, and 1971-78, to make a more sensitive examination as well as to compare them with Value Line betas available only for 1971-78. For k_e with historical growth, we have also drawn a graph with nine-quarter moving averages to dampen the sharp fluctuations caused by the use of quarterly historical data. The resultant smoother fluctuations should normally make it easier to see the underlying trends.

The third method deals with earnings-price ratios for 1965-78 (see Figures 6.24-6.41). The graphs and trend lines of the average of all groups as well as for each group are of the same types as those done for the cost of equity capital with forward-looking growth.

The fourth method looks at the betas of the CAPM during the period 1971-78. Figures 6.42-6.57 have been prepared for this method as well.

On every figure, time will be shown on the horizontal axis, while k_e, earnings-price ratio, and beta values will be represented on the vertical axis. Unless the contrary is stated, continuous lines or curves indicate multinational values, while dotted ones represent domestic values.

After the figures pertaining to one of the above mentioned methods have been shown, there will be summary tables listing the results of the three tests for each of the four methods. For instance, the first method, which uses the cost of equity capital with forward-looking growth, has first been tested for the percentage of points lying between $\hat{s}$, the standard error around the trend line. Thus, Table 6.1 shows the results for the average of all groups as well as for each industry group for both the multinationals and the domestics. Table 6.2 shows the results of the paired-difference test and the trend significance test and their respective confidence levels. This process has been repeated for each method (see Tables 6.4-6.7). As already mentioned, the second method will only have results for the averages of all groups (see Table 6.3).

Finally, Tables 6.8 and 6.9 show the test results for the averages of all groups for all four methods. This should facilitate their comparisons.

FIGURE 6.1. k_e with Forward-looking Growth (average of all groups)

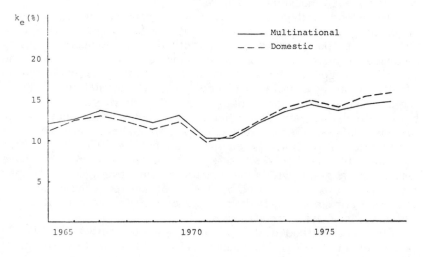

FIGURE 6.2. k_e with Forward-looking Growth Trend Line (average of all groups)

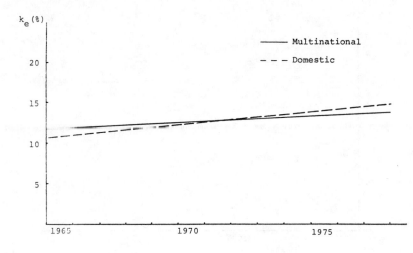

FIGURE 6.3. k_e with Forward-looking Growth Trend Line – 1965-70 (average of all groups)

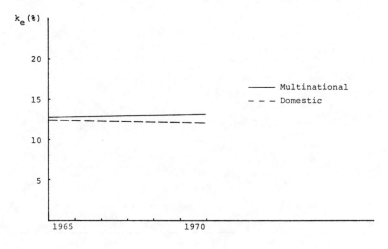

FIGURE 6.4. k_e with Forward-looking Growth Trend Line – 1971-78 (average of all groups)

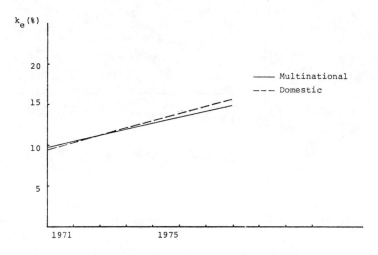

FIGURE 6.5. k_e with Forward-looking Growth – Petroleum Refining

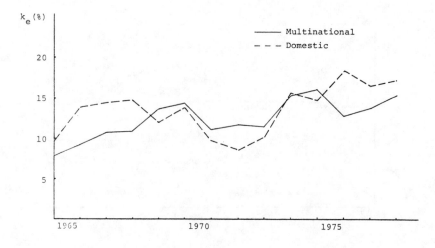

FIGURE 6.6. k_e with Forward-looking Growth Trend Line – Petroleum Refining

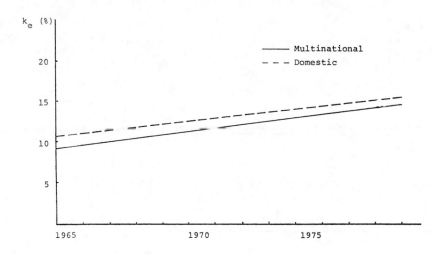

FIGURE 6.7. k_e with Forward-looking Growth – Electrical Machinery

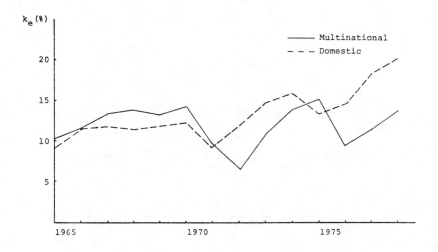

FIGURE 6.8. k_e with Forward-looking Growth Trend Line – Electrical Machinery

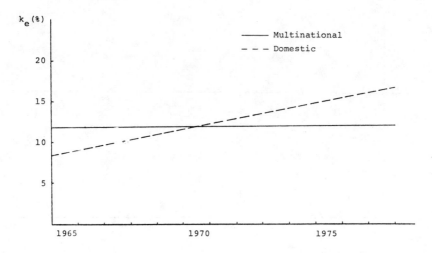

FIGURE 6.9. k_e with Forward-looking Growth – Nonelectrical Machinery

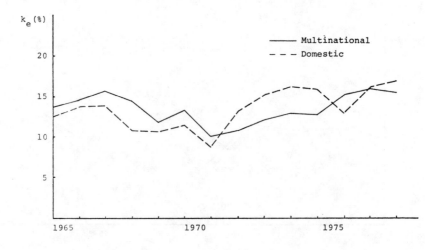

FIGURE 6.10. k_e with Forward-looking Growth Trend Line–Nonelectrical Machinery

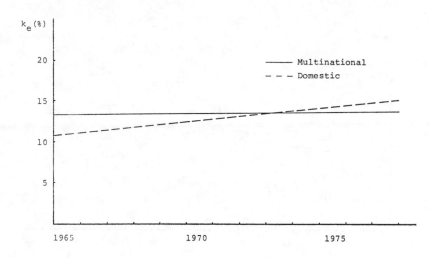

FIGURE 6.11. k_e with Forward-looking Growth – Chemical and Allied Products

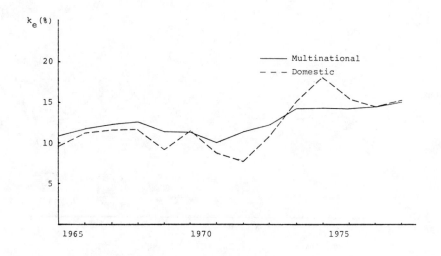

FIGURE 6.12. k_e with Forward-looking Growth Trend Line – Chemical and Allied Products

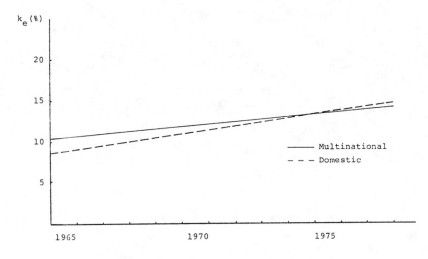

FIGURE 6.13. k_e with Forward-looking Growth – Fabricated Metal Products

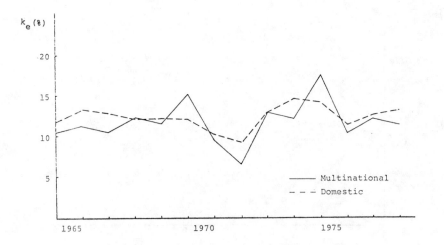

FIGURE 6.14. k_e with Forward-looking Growth Trend Line – Fabricated Metal Products

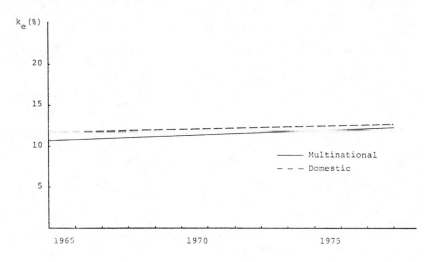

FIGURE 6.15. k_e with Forward-looking Growth – Nonferrous Metals

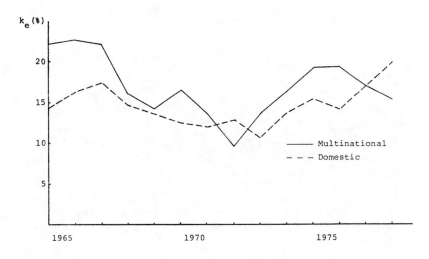

FIGURE 6.16. k_e with Forward-looking Growth Trend Line – Nonferrous Metals

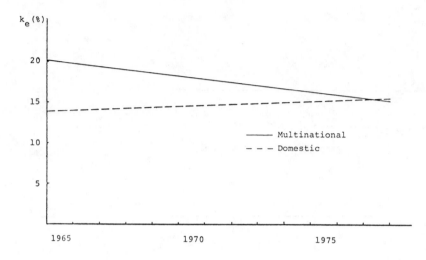

FIGURE 6.17. k_e with Forward-looking Growth – Food Products

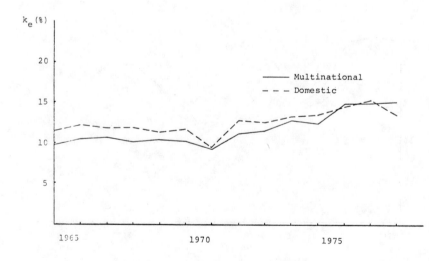

FIGURE6.18.k$_e$withForward-lookingGrowthTrendLine—FoodProducts

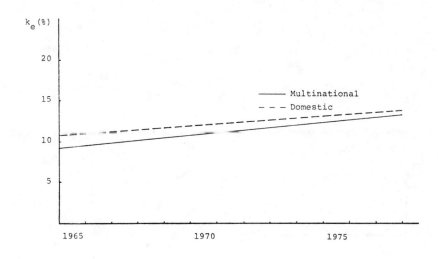

FIGURE 6.19. k$_e$ with Historical Growth (average of all groups)

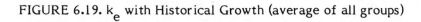

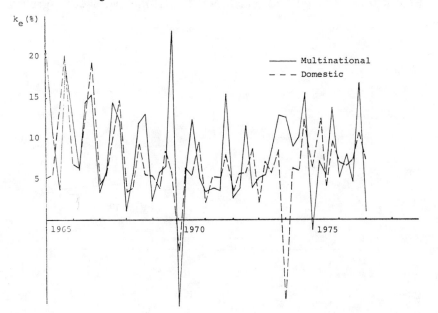

FIGURE 6.20. k_e with Historical Growth: Nine-Quarter Moving Average (average of all groups)

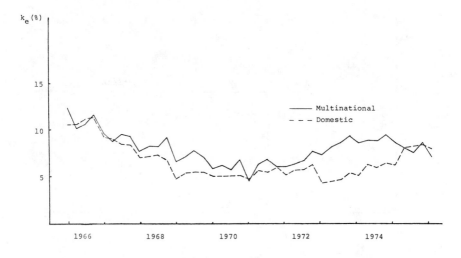

FIGURE 6.21. k_e with Historical Growth Trend Line (average of all groups)

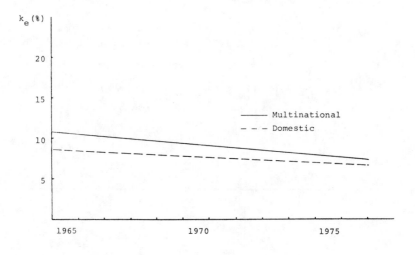

FIGURE 6.22. k_e with Historical Growth Trend Line – 1965-70 (average of all groups)

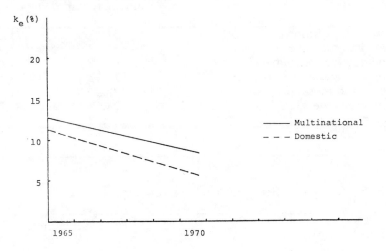

FIGURE 6.23. k_e with Historical Growth Trend Line – 1971-76 (average of all groups)

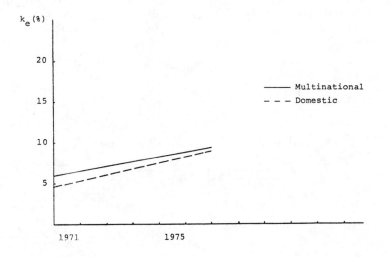

TABLE 6.1. k_e with Forward-looking Growth

Industrial Group	Percentage of Points between ŝ	
	Multinational	Domestic
Petroleum refining	57.14	71.43
Electrical machinery	78.57	71.43
Nonelectrical machinery	64.29	71.43
Chemical and allied products	71.43	78.57
Fabricated metal products	78.57	71.43
Nonferrous metals	78.57	64.29
Food products	64.29	78.57
All groups	78.57	71.43

TABLE 6.2. k_e with Forward-looking Growth

Industrial Group	Paired Difference		Trend Significance	
	t Value	α	t Value	α
Petroleum refining	6.23	.01	-.12	n.s.[a]
Electrical machinery	4.89	.01	3.65	.01
Nonelectrical machinery	6.38	.01	3.33	.01
Chemical and allied products	3.68	.01	1.645	.20
Fabricated metal products	5.35	.01	.669	n.s.[a]
Nonferrous metals	5.71	.01	2.413	.05
Food products	8.10	.01	2.324[b]	.05
All groups	8.65	.01	5.116	.01

[a] n.s. = not significant.

[b] Contrary to hypothesis.

TABLE 6.3. k_e with Historical Growth (all groups)

Percentage of Points between ŝ	
Multinational	Domestic
75.51	81.63

Paired Difference		Trend Significance	
t Value	α	t Value	α
7.03	.01	.111	n.s.*

*n.s. = not significant.

A look at the graphs and summary tables of k_e with forward-looking growth shows us that the results essentially support our original hypothesis; that is, the cost of equity capital of U.S. multinational firms has decreased in relation to that of the U.S. domestic firms during the period under study.

The percentage of points lying between the standard error around the trend line is definitely acceptable for the average of all groups, as shown in Table 6.1. As we have already mentioned in Chapter 3, ideally 68 percent or more of the points should lie between these standard error lines. We have 78.57 percent and 71.43 percent respectively for the multinational average of all groups and the domestic average of all groups. All the industry groups, except petroleum refining, yield acceptable results. Only in a few cases do they have a 64.29 percent, which is quite close to 68 percent. Petroleum refining has a low 57.14 percent for the multinationals and 71.43 percent for the domestics. Thus, the results are generally acceptable.

The paired-difference test demonstrates that there is definitely a highly significant difference between the multinationals and the domestics. This is true for both the average of all groups and for each industry group. They are all significant at $\alpha = .01$ or a confidence level of 99 percent.

Finally, the trend significance test shows that the trend of the difference between the multinationals and the domestics significantly ($\alpha = .01$) supports our hypothesis for the average of all groups. The only group that shows a result contrary to our hypothesis is food products with $\alpha = .05$. Petroleum refining and fabricated metal products do not yield difference trends that are significantly different from 0. Electrical machinery, nonelectrical machinery, chemical and allied products, and nonferrous metals are in line with our hypothesis with respective α's of .01, .01, .20, and .05.

Thus, the results generally lend considerable support to the hypothesis. Of course, one cannot claim that such results give an absolute proof of the validity of the hypothesis. Rather, one could say that these results increase the likelihood of the validity of the hypothesis.

The cost of equity capital with historical growth (calculated according to the Kohers method as explained in Chapter 3) yields positive results for the percentage of points lying between the standard error around the trend line and the paired-difference test. However, the difference between multinationals and domestics does not have a significant trend as may be observed in Table 6.3. To an important extent, this insignificance is due to the sharp fluctuations of k_e values during the period. This shows how much change can result from a different growth rate calculation method (see Chapter 8 for a more detailed analysis).

FIGURE 6.24. Earnings-Price Ratios (average of all groups)

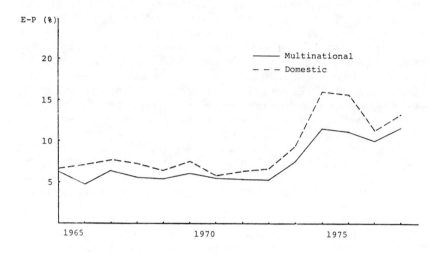

FIGURE 6.25. Earnings-Price Ratios Trend Line (average of all groups)

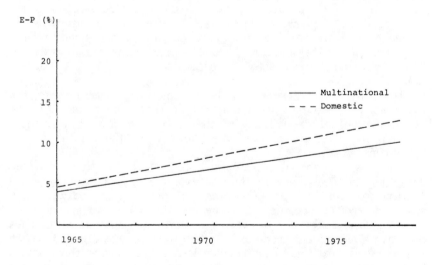

FIGURE 6.26. Earnings-Price Ratios Trend Line – 1965-70 (average of all groups)

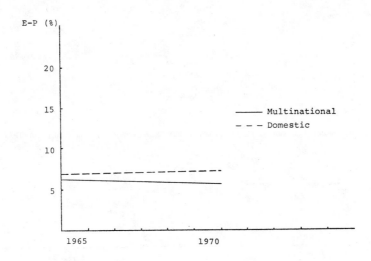

FIGURE 6.27. Earnings-Price Ratios Trend Line – 1971-78 (average of all groups)

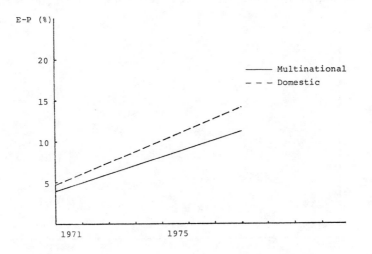

FIGURE 6.28. Earnings-Price Ratios – Petroleum Refining

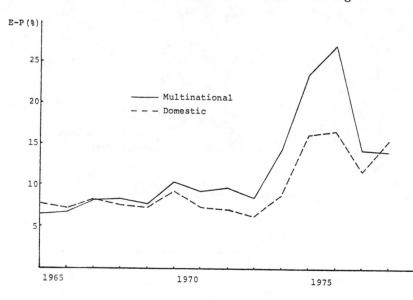

FIGURE 6.29. Earnings-Price Ratios Trend Line – Petroleum Refining

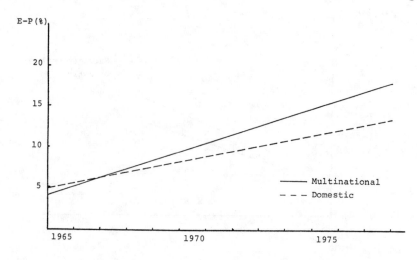

FIGURE 6.30. Earnings-Price Ratios – Electrical Machinery

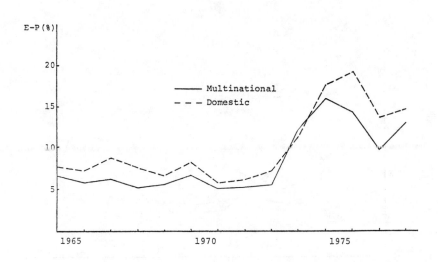

FIGURE 6.31. Earnings-Price Ratios Trend Line – Electrical Machinery

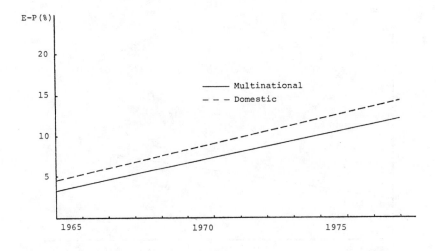

FIGURE 6.32. Earnings-Price Ratios – Nonelectrical Machinery

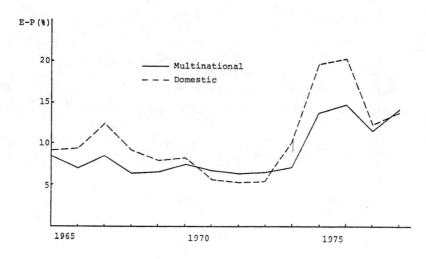

FIGURE 6.33. Earnings-Price Ratios Trend Line – Nonelectrical Machinery

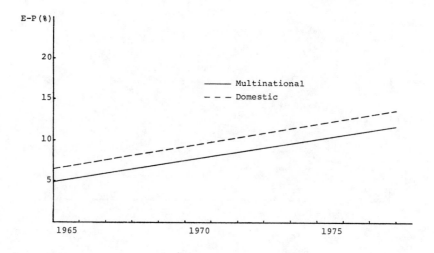

FIGURE 6.34. Earnings-Price Ratios – Chemical and Allied Products

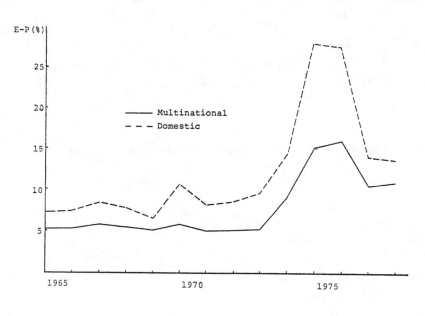

FIGURE 6.35. Earnings-Price Ratios Trend Line – Chemical and Allied Products

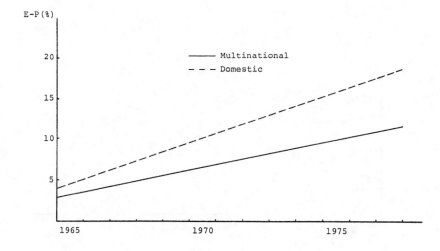

FIGURE 6.36. Earnings-Price Ratios – Fabricated Metal Products

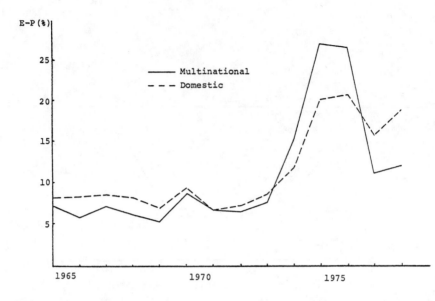

FIGURE 6.37. Earnings-Price Ratios Trend Line – Fabricated Metal Product

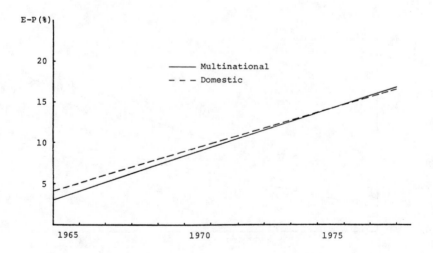

FIGURE 6.38. Earnings-Price Ratios – Nonferrous Metals

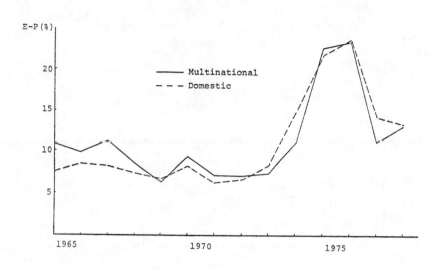

FIGURE 6.39. Earnings-Price Ratios Trend Line – Nonferrous Metals

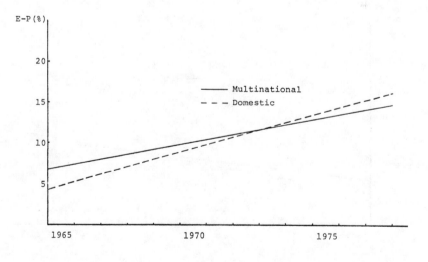

FIGURE 6.40. Earnings-Price Ratios – Food Products

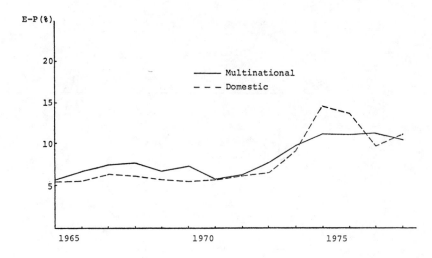

FIGURE 6.41. Earnings-Price Ratios Trend Line – Food Products

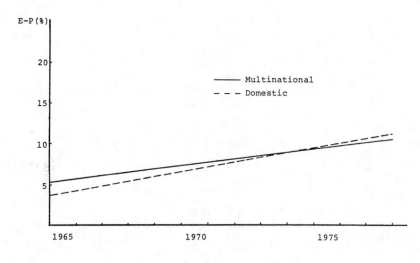

TABLE 6.4. Earnings-Price Ratios

Industrial Group	Percentage of Points between $	
	Multinational	Domestic
Petroleum refining	85.71	78.57
Electrical machinery	71.43	78.57
Nonelectrical machinery	64.29	64.29
Chemical and allied products	78.57	85.71
Fabricated metal products	85.71	71.43
Nonferrous metals	85.71	85.71
Food products	64.29	85.71
All groups	71.43	85.71

TABLE 6.5. Earnings-Price Ratios

Industrial Group	Paired Difference		Trend Significance	
	t Value	α	t Value	α
Petroleum refining	3.330	.01	2.008[a]	.10
Electrical machinery	5.960	.01	.935	n.s.[b]
Nonelectrical machinery	4.960	.01	.102	n.s.[b]
Chemical and allied products	4.740	.01	2.006	.10
Fabricated metal products	4.210	.01	.426	n.s.[b]
Nonferrous metals	4.300	.01	3.809	.01
Food products	4.980	.01	1.538	.20
All groups	4.910	.01	1.580	.20

[a]Contrary to hypothesis.

[b]n.s. = not significant.

The average for all groups of the earnings-price ratios yields results that support the hypothesis. The percentage of points lying between the standard error lines around the trend are 71.43 and 85.71 percent respectively for the multinational firms and domestic firms. The paired-difference test is significant at a confidence level of 99 percent (α = .01), while there is an 80 percent (α = .20) confidence level for the trend significance test.

When the industry groups are looked at separately, the percentages of points between the standard error lines around the trend are satisfactory. Only nonelectrical machinery and food products have values of 64.29 percent. The other groups have values ranging from 71.43 percent and 85.71 percent. The paired-difference test shows that all groups are significantly different at a confidence level of 99 percent (α = .01). Three groups yield trend significance test results that support the hypothesis. These are chemical and allied products, nonferrous metals, and food products with respective confidence levels of 90 percent, 99 percent, and 80 percent. The results for electrical machinery, nonelectrical machinery, and fabricated metal products are not significant. One group, petroleum refining, has a trend that is significant at a 90 percent confidence level. However, the trend of this group runs against the hypothesis. Briefly, there are three groups that support the hypothesis, one that goes against it, and three that are insignificant.

In general, the results of the earnings-price ratios support the hypothesis although not as strongly as those of the cost of equity capital with forward-looking growth rates. As will be explained in the next chapter, economic and political developments of a general nature as well as more specific ones are likely to influence earnings-price ratios more rapidly and in a more pronounced manner than they influence the cost of equity capital figures with forward-looking growth rates. The latter try to take into account long-term trends in addition to immediate developments.

FIGURE 6.42. CAPM Betas (average of all groups)

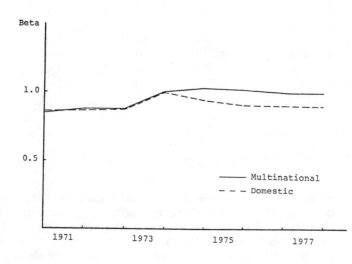

FIGURE 6.43. CAPM Betas Trend Line (average of all groups)

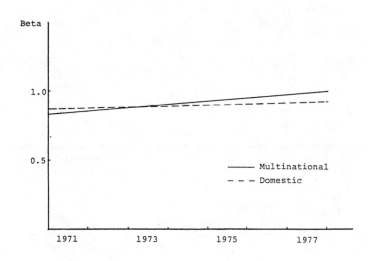

FIGURE 6.44. CAPM Betas – Petroleum Refining

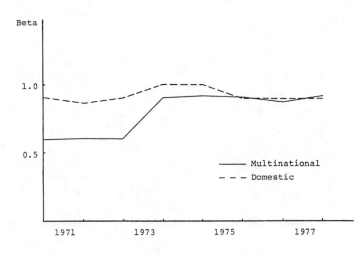

FIGURE 6.45. CAPM Betas Trend Line – Petroleum Refining

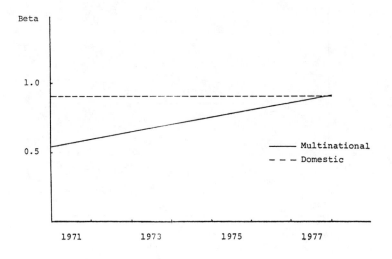

FIGURE 6.46. CAPM Betas – Electrical Machinery

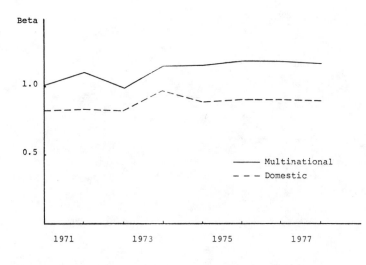

FIGURE 6.47. CAPM Betas Trend Line – Electrical Machinery

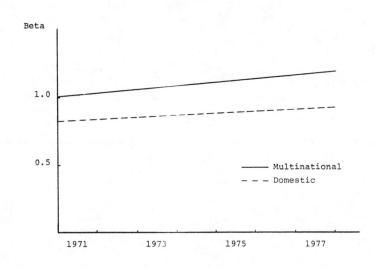

FIGURE 6.48. CAPM Betas – Nonelectrical Machinery

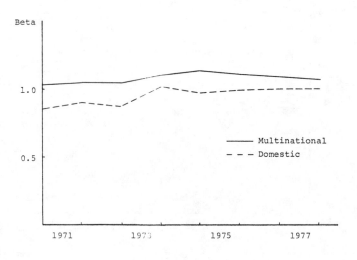

FIGURE 6.49. CAPM Betas Trend Line – Nonelectrical Machinery

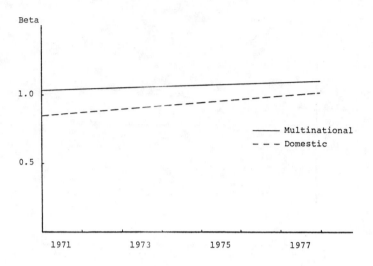

FIGURE 6.50. CAPM Betas – Chemical and Allied Products

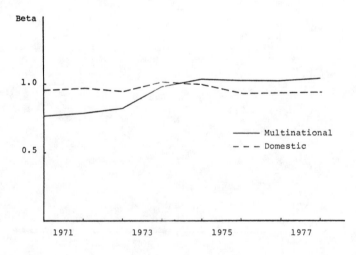

FIGURE 6.51. CAPM Betas Trend Line – Chemical and Allied Products

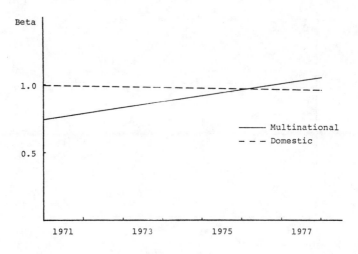

FIGURE 6.52. CAPM Betas – Fabricated Metal Products

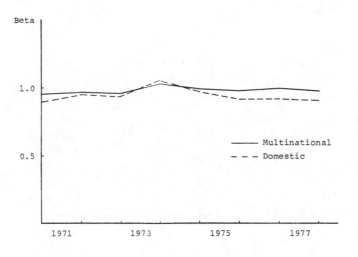

FIGURE 6.53. CAPM Betas Trend Line – Fabricated Metal Products

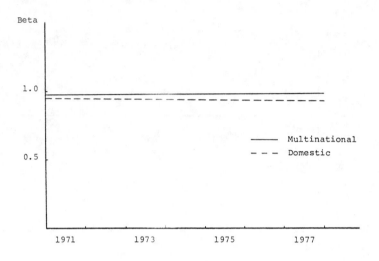

FIGURE 6.54. CAPM Betas – Nonferrous Metals

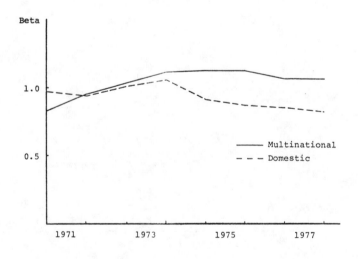

FIGURE 6.55. CAPM Betas Trend Line – Nonferrous Metals

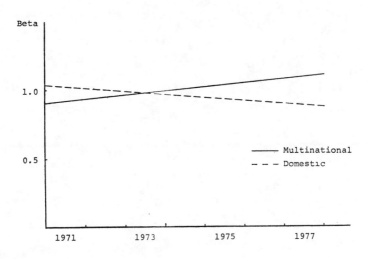

FIGURE 6.56. CAPM Betas – Food Products

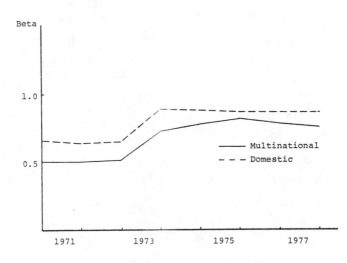

FIGURE 6.57. CAPM Betas Trend Line – Food Products

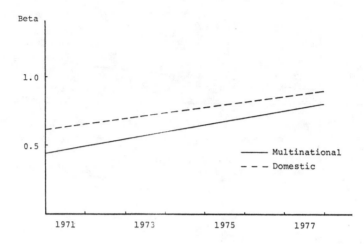

TABLE 6.6. CAPM Betas

Industrial Group	Percentage of Points between §	
	Multinational	Domestic
Petroleum refining	75.0	75.0
Electrical machinery	62.5	87.5
Nonelectrical machinery	87.5	87.5
Chemical and allied products	75.0	87.5
Fabricated metal products	87.5	87.5
Nonferrous metals	87.5	62.5
Food products	62.5	75.0
All groups	75.0	87.5

TABLE 6.7. CAPM Betas

Industrial Group	Paired Difference		Trend Significance	
	t Value	α	t Value	α
Petroleum refining	3.186	.02	24.240	.01
Electrical machinery	13.210	.01	.852	n.s.*
Nonelectrical machinery	7.890	.01	2.470	.05
Chemical and allied products	5.690	.01	4.327	.01
Fabricated metal products	4.830	.01	1.347	n.s.*
Nonferrous metals	4.030	.01	4.260	.01
Food products	10.820	.01	1.750	.20
All groups	3.850	.01	3.678	.01

*n.s. = not significant.

An examination of Figure 6.42 shows that the average beta value of all groups for the multinationals goes together with that of the domestics until the end of 1973. After that, the two averages fork out with the multinational betas becoming higher in relation to domestic ones. Thus, we see that systematic risk, which was about the same for both until 1973, becomes different after that. The explanation of this phenomenon lies in the degree of interrelationship of the economies of world countries.

Rugman (1979, pp. 63-67) looks at the issue through the interrelation of world equity markets, which became very strong after 1972. Wood and Jianakoplos (1979, pp. 47-55) examine the annual percentage change of the gross domestic products of the United States, the United Kingdom, Canada, France, Germany, Italy, and Japan. As Figure 6.58 indicates, starting from 1973, there has been a greater similarity in rates of growth of output among the major industrialized countries. One can easily conclude that this situation left less room for international diversification and hence considerably less possibilities for the reduction of systematic risk. This is a very probable explanation for the relative increase in the systematic risk of the multinational firms after 1973.

If there were less covariation of national economies before 1973 than after, then one would expect returns from multinationals before 1973 to exhibit a lower covariance with the U.S. market index than they do afterward. It may be assumed that domestic returns have the same covariance with the U.S. market index before and after 1973. Hence, the betas of the multinationals should rise in relation to those of the domestics. The formulation for beta should make it more evident:

$$\text{Beta} = \frac{\text{Covariance } (r_m, R_f)}{\sigma_m^{\,2}}$$

where r_m, R_f, and $\sigma_m^{\,2}$ respectively denote the market return, the risk free rate of return, and the variance of the market returns. Still, this relative increase of multinational betas should not be taken as a refutation of the basic hypothesis of this study. Insofar as the value of diversification properties per se of overseas investment have decreased, one would expect the cost of equity capital of multinationals to rise in relation to that of domestics. The fact that this is not the case indicates that other factors affecting total risk have swamped the changed diversification potential. It was stated in Chapter 3 that betas explain only about 30 percent of total risk, and for some stocks the beta values give a very limited explanation of price fluctuations. Thus, it is quite possible to have a quite risky share with a beta value of .50. Fogler (1978, pp. 109-32) shows that the method of computation of betas can drastically alter results, such that by one method the beta value may be higher for Firm A than for Firm B, while the reverse will be true with another method or methods. Also, a fundamental assumption of the capital asset pricing model is perfect markets. The stagflation, which set in after 1973, did not look like a propitious time to have perfect markets.

FIGURE 6.58. Gross Domestic Product in Seven Industrialized Countries

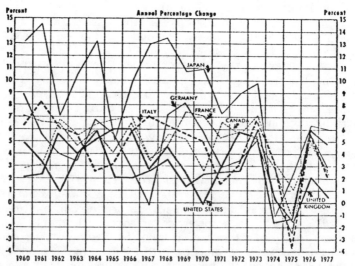

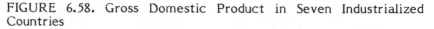

Source: Wood, G. E., and N. A. Jianakoplos. 1979. "Coordinated International Economic Expansion: Are Convoys or Locomotives the Answer?" In International Business - 1979. A Selection of Current Readings, edited by D. A. Anderson, M. Luqmani, and Z. A. Quareshi, p. 47. East Lansing: Michigan State University Press.

Other than international diversification, one should also look at export diversification. While Hirsch and Lev (1971) show how exports diversification can be beneficial for companies, Pras (1980, pp. 32-37) writes that for large firms, such as those in our sample, export diversification plays a more important role than product diversification, which has a negligible influence. Export diversification is of greater importance for the domestic firms in our sample since they either have no plants abroad or have them on a much lesser scale than the multinationals. An examination based on the reports of some companies in our sample and supplemented by phone calls shows that the domestics were greater exporters, directly from the United States, than were the multinationals. Except for petroleum refining, which may be more dependent on product diversification, the other industries – chemical and allied products – that run contrary to our hypothesis seem to have domestics benefiting more from export diversification than the multinationals. However, the reader should be cautioned that data could not be obtained for all firms, and for those that were obtained, a range of values or simply ordinal, rather than cardinal, information was frequently received. This was due to the reticence of many firms to give out such information.

It can be seen from Table 6.6 that the percentages of points lying between the standard error lines around the trend are respectively 75.0 percent and 87.5 percent for the averages of all groups of the multinationals and the domestics. Individual industry groups, too, show satisfactory results with values of 62.5, 75.0, and 87.5 percent.

Table 6.7 indicates that the paired-difference test yields highly significant results for the average of all groups as well as for the individual groups. With the exception of petroleum refining, where there is a significant difference between multinational betas and domestic betas at a confidence level of 98 percent, all the results are significant at a confidence level of 99 percent.

As for the trend significance test, results generally show that the systematic risk of multinationals has increased in relation to that of the domestics. The average of all groups shows that this trend is significant at a confidence level of 99 percent. Petroleum refining, chemical and allied products, nonferrous metals, and food products are significant at confidence levels of 99, 99, 99, and 80 percent respectively. Nonelectrical machinery displays an opposite trend at a 95 percent confidence level, while electrical machinery and fabricated metal products do not have trends that are significantly different for the multinationals and the domestics.

In this study, the betas are not used to prove or disprove the hypothesis but are simply an extension that shows how the systematic, not total, risk of multinationals fared in relation to that of the domestics. Obviously, the CAPM cost of equity capital based on these betas will give us the same ordinal results since, by formulation, the two are positively correlated (see Chapter 3).

The results for the average of all groups using the four different methods are shown in Tables 6.8 and 6.9.

TABLE 6.8. Results for Averages of All Groups

Test	Percentage of Points between §	
	Multinational	Domestic
k_e with forward-looking growth	78.57	71.43
k_e with historical growth	75.51	81.63
Earnings-price ratios	71.43	85.71
CAPM betas	75.00	87.50

TABLE 6.7. CAPM Betas

Test	Paired Difference		Trend Significance	
	t Value	α	t Value	α
k_e with forward-looking growth	8.650	.01	5.116	.01
k_e with historical growth	7.030	.01	.111	n.s.*
Earnings-price ratios	4.910	.01	1.580	.20
CAPM betas	3.850	.01	3.678	.01

*n.s. = not significant.

7

An Analysis
of Industry Groups

The purpose of this chapter is to analyze each industry group result separately and on a yearly basis in the light of ex ante and ex post information obtained primarily from the U.S. Industrial Outlook (yearly from 1965 to 1978), Value Line Investment Survey reports, and Standard & Poor's Industry Surveys. All three are continuously updated reports trying to predict what the prospects for a certain industry are in advance (ex ante). For instance, the U.S. Industrial Outlook of 1965, which was actually prepared in 1964 tried to predict the prospects (sales growth, profitability, stability, etc.) for, say, the chemical and allied products for 1965 and even further. Of course, the predictions may or may not be equal to what actually occurs later (ex post). However, ex ante estimations are particularly important since investors normally use this information, among other sources, when buying stocks. Factors such as expected growth in earnings, sales, or stability will have an important influence on earnings-price ratios. Besides these three major sources, reference was also made to company reports, which sometimes tried to predict the prospects of the industry group to which the company belonged. However, such reports were frequently too optimistic for obvious reasons. Hence, the main emphasis was placed on the above three sources, which rarely contradicted one another in their predictions for the same year. All three sources are heavily used by investors, and thus their predictions are very likely to be quite close to those of investors who buy stocks. Also, they complement one another. For instance, Standard & Poor's Industry Surveys gives substantial and systematic information on petroleum refining, chemical and allied products, fabricated metal products, and food products but is

95

rather scanty and unsystematic when it comes to the other three groups. On the other hand, U.S. Industrial Outlook gives little or no information on petroleum refining. Value Line Investment Survey provides complementary information in quite a number of instances. In view of the information and predictions given by these sources, possible and plausible explanations are presented for each industry group results as shown in the previous chapter.

It must be stressed that the analysis will be carried out for the earnings-price ratios (E-Ps), since it is possible to relate these to the information given by the above sources. E-Ps are usually influenced clearly in the short-term by general as well as specific developments, namely those pertaining to an industry or a company. It is therefore possible to show, to a certain extent at least, the relationship between these developments and the E-Ps. On the other hand, the cost of equity capital calculations, as described in Chapter 3, are based on long-term forward-looking growth rates calculated by the Value Line Investment Survey according to a method that they only partially explain. Without knowing what Value Line's analysts had in mind when calculating these ex ante growth rates for the coming 3 to 5 years, it becomes a virtual impossibility to explain the significance of these results as an immediate reflection of developments as we have attempted to do for E-Ps. Still, because of the statistical law of large numbers, upon which our significance tests in the previous chapter rely, some conclusions can be reached for the entire 1965-78 period.

Unless thoroughly familiar with the recent economic history of the United States and its implications for stock prices, the reader is urged to read the appendix, Major Economic Events (1965-78), before and/or while reading the explanations to be given for the yearly changes in the E-Ps of each industry group. The reader should also note that the comparative multinational-domestic E-Ps graph of a group has been placed after its year-by-year analysis.

PETROLEUM REFINING

At the end of 1964 and the beginning of 1965, multinational oil firms were more vulnerable to international competition compared to the domestic oil companies, which were protected by import quota restrictions. Competition for the multinationals arose mainly from Soviet oil barter for British and Japanese manufactured products. Still, both multinationals and domestic expected sales and net income growth above the average of all stocks. Although it was expected that the U.S. dollar would be devalued, this was not likely to make U.S. domestic firms competitive to foreign oil in world markets. The 7.4 percent devaluation was far from being sufficient to make up for the large price per barrel difference between domestic and foreign oil, which stood respectively at $3.00 and

$1.85. One can say that, overall, 1965 gave somewhat better prospects for domestic oil, which was protected by import quotas, as opposed to foreign oil, which had to face international competition. This is a very probable explanation for the domestic earnings-price ratio decrease in relation to the multinationals.

At the beginning of 1966, the growth in earnings of domestic firms was expected to ease somewhat. At the same time, the profits of multinationals suffered due to weak prices and higher taxes in Libya, which even planned to raise them somewhat more. These are very likely explanations for the rises in E-Ps for both multinationals and domestics, though the latter's rose at a slower rate, probably because investors perceived it as more immune to international conjectures.

While U.S. domestic oil prices were firm, those abroad were depressed in 1966, and competition in international markets was quite severe. Thus, domestics had better prospects than multinationals had for making larger profits in 1967. Host countries were seeking a larger share of profits than before. In 1967, the E-Ps of domestics fell, while those of multinationals rose slightly. The Arab-Israeli war of June 1967 was another factor that worked against the multinationals.

In 1968, prospects for the multinationals were improving even more than those of the domestics. Multinationals were able to resolve the supply and transportations problems caused by the 1967 Arab-Israeli war. Refined petroleum prices in most parts of the world increased. While earnings were expected to grow in 1968, there were still some uncertainties as to prices and taxes. The E-Ps of multinationals fell slightly faster than those of domestics.

The expected demand slump for 1969 made investors wary about both multinational and domestic oil firms. However, there were prospects for large oil and natural gas discoveries in Alaska. This could have been a factor that made domestic E-Ps rise less quickly than multinational E-Ps.

Although the prospects for 1970 were not too good either, earnings fell faster than prices, resulting in lower E-Ps for both domestics and multinationals. Yet, the multinational E-Ps declined more slowly because of Middle East oil uncertainties caused by events such as the May 1970 sabotage of the Trans Arabian Pipeline, which brought some 450,000 barrels per day of Saudi oil to the Mediterranean Sea.

The relative stock prices of both multinational and domestic firms deteriorated during 1971. However, that of multinationals declined faster because of the uncertainty created by Libya's imposition of extra taxes on its crude production. Other oil-producing countries followed Libya's example.

Earnings were expected to be modest in 1972 for multinationals. However, although it later did not turn out that way, negotiations between multinationals and OPEC seemed to take a more optimistic turn. The decline of multinational E-Ps exceeded that of the domestic E-Ps. The relatively warm U.S. winter of 1972 reduced oil prices.

Toward the end of 1973, the Arab oil embargo allowed oil companies, especially multinationals, to earn very high profits.

At the end of 1973 and during 1974, skyrocketing earnings coupled with uncertainties, which kept oil stock prices lower than warranted, tremendously increased the E-Ps, especially those of the multinationals, which seemed more vulnerable to world political conjectures. In one year foreign oil prices went up by about 350 percent, while domestic oil prices increased by about 200 percent. During 1974, domestic oil profit prospects looked better than those of multinationals to be subjected to windfall profits taxes.

Due to the uncertainties on the world political scene in 1975, investors found domestic oil stocks more reliable than multinational ones, and the E-Ps of the former increased only slightly during the year. Despite increasing oil prices, the relative inelasticity of oil demand made it fall by only 5 percent. Another factor that made multinationals look worse than the domestics was President Ford's intention to impose a tariff on imported oil.

While oil earnings began to decline in 1976, investors expected that they would soon go up again. This made prices go up while earnings declined. However, earnings did not go up as expected, and this resulted in a rapid fall of E-Ps for both multinationals and domestics. The decrease of uncertainties in foreign oil supplies led to an even more rapid decrease in the E-Ps of multinationals as compared to the domestics.

FIGURE 7.1. Earnings-Price Ratios – Petroleum Refining

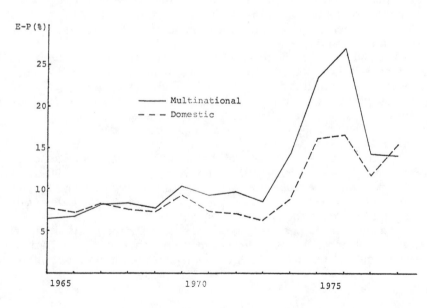

During 1977, foreign oil uncertainties began to subside, while the world economic outlook had become brighter at the end of 1976. Oil demand did not fall as much as previously thought. At the same time, strong price controls for U.S. domestic oil made it less attractive to investors. During the year, the domestic E-Ps rose rather sharply, while the multinational E-Ps fell slightly.

ELECTRICAL MACHINERY

Relatively good profit and sales increases realized in 1964 led investors to believe that these would continue in 1965. Thus, the E-Ps of both multinationals and domestic somewhat declined during 1965.

Despite good prospects during 1966, E-Ps increased because earnings increased faster than prices. The real boom was for color television tubes, but this does not affect results of this study since none of the companies in the sample dealt with television tubes. Multinationals did better in their foreign than in their domestic operations. This is a probable reason for the slower rise of multi-national E-Ps compared to domestic E-Ps during 1966.

In 1967, the whole electrical machinery industry was in a boom, and prospects looked bright. Despite substantial increases in earnings, prices increased even faster, thus leading to a fall in the E-Ps of both multinationals and domestics.

Prospects were moderately favorable in 1968. Yet E-Ps were too low probably because electrical machinery shares were popular with institutional investors. While multinationals were partly sheltered from a 10 percent corporate surtax, foreign markets became more competitive compared to the previous year. In the end, multi-national E-Ps rose while domestic ones declined.

During 1969, there were two probable reasons for the rise in E-Ps for both multinationals and domestics. First, earnings increased faster than prices. Also, toward the end of the year, defense cuts and a less buoyant U.S. economy could have contributed to the rise in E-Ps.

Net incomes did not keep pace with sales during 1970, and profitability fell steadily while E-Ps declined. At the same time, because investors anticipated a good future for the electrical machinery industry, prices for these shares rose sharply. The multi-national E-Ps decline was slower probably because of competition in foreign markets.

Although the situation was good in 1971, investors had already anticipated that in 1970, and stock prices did not increase substantially during 1971. Both multinational and domestic E-Ps were relative stable.

During 1972, despite generally higher sales, earnings were declining as a result of keen competition within the temporarily declining U.S. market due to reduced capital spending by the electrical machinery sector. As demand was better abroad, multinational E-Ps were relatively stable while the domestic ones rose.

Disappointment, resulting from the low earnings of 1972, caused a fall in prices in 1973. However, earnings picked up during the year without a corresponding increase in prices. This trend, coupled with the world recession in the last quarter of 1973, caused a high jump in both domestic and multinational E-Ps. The higher rise of multinational E-Ps was probably due to economic uncertainties throughout the world.

In 1974, there was a peak demand for semiconductors. However, none of the firms in our sample was involved in that and, thus, they could not benefit from this event. The E-Ps kept rising fast during the year. It was a slower rise for the multinationals, which found a new market among the newly richer oil producers.

At the end of 1974 and during 1975, there was a demand drop for the U.S. market for electrical machinery resulting from a drop in construction activity and a drop in demand for generation equipment used by utilities. Foreign sales of multinationals continued to increase. During 1975, the multinational E-Ps fell while the domestic ones rose.

The domestic stagnation of 1975 ended in 1976, and total industry sales were expected to expand by at least 8 percent since the housing sector was rapidly recovering. Price increases coupled with lower interest rates led to higher earnings and better prospects. This, in turn, led to a rapid decline in E-Ps for both domestics and multinationals.

FIGURE 7.2. Earnings-Price Ratios – Electrical Machinery

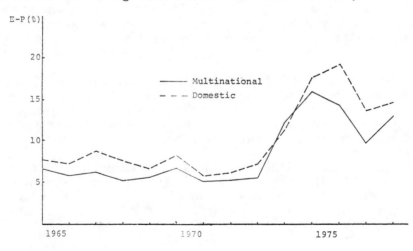

After the strong rebound of profits in 1976, the following year witnessed a slowing down in sales of electrical machinery. The situation was made worse for multinationals, which had their foreign earnings negatively influenced by a wave of currency revaluations against the U.S. dollar. Thus, while the E-Ps of both domestics and multinationals rose, the latter's rose even faster.

NONELECTRICAL MACHINERY

During 1965, prospects were rather good for nonelectrical machinery. They were much better for the multinationals, which found high demands for their products. While the domestic E-Ps rose slightly, the multinational ones fell considerably.

Although there was a glimpse of promise at the beginning of 1966, tight money policy during the first half of the year in the United States and then the suspension of the 7 percent tax credit made these shares, especially the domestic ones that were more affected, less attractive to investors. While the E-Ps of both types of firms rose, the domestic ones rose even faster.

Despite the off-and-on tight money policy, 1967 looked promising for the machinery industry because of good backlogs and spending projects. Earnings showed rapid increases in the first half of the year, and this was translated into even more rapid price increases. Both multinational and domestic E-Ps fell. The latter did so at a faster pace.

Earnings began to slow down in the U.S. market during 1968. However, sales grew at a faster rate overseas. Yet this was not translated into lower E-Ps for the multinationals. A probable reason might have been investors' anxiety over the reduction of plant expansions abroad. While the multinational E-Ps remained relatively stable, domestic E-Ps fell during 1968.

Earnings were expected to increase during 1969 and they did. Prices also went up but at a slower rate. Even prospects of a slowdown in the U.S. economy did not seem to deter investors from going to domestic shares. As the demand for petroleum products rose, there was a corresponding increase in the demand for oil-drilling machines. The increase in E-Ps was very slight for the domestics and moderate for the multinationals.

Despite some gloom over the cooling economy and rising un-employment, which negatively influenced stock prices at the beginning of 1970, the second half of the year witnessed a rise in machinery share prices, especially domestic ones. Domestic E-Ps fell even faster than multinational ones.

The Value Line predicted a general drop in earnings for 1971. While this decline materialized for some firms, the majority either remained stable or even increased their earnings. Good prospects in oil- and water-drilling equipment as well as in construction machinery prevented share price decreases. Both multinational and domestic E-Ps fell slightly during the year.

In 1972, while the demand for energy and construction equipment rose, capital spending by manufacturing companies was somewhat slower. E-Ps for both multinationals and domestics remained stable.

During 1973, earnings rose substantially without a corresponding increase in prices mainly because of the fear of possible shortages in raw materials, particularly of basic metals in the United States. The multinationals were less affected because the devaluation of the dollar made them more competitive abroad. While multinational E-Ps increased moderately, domestic ones rose sharply.

Despite steady earnings, machinery share prices declined very much, probably because of the pessimism caused by the energy crisis and the economic recession in 1974. During the year, the E-Ps of both multinationals and domestics grew very rapidly.

Although there were bleak prospects at the beginning of 1975, nonelectrical machinery earnings grew at a 13 percent annual rate during the last quarter of the year. Also, share prices went up considerably. The rise in E-Ps for both multinationals and domestics continued but at a far more moderate rate.

FIGURE 7.3. Earnings-Price Ratios – Nonelectrical Machinery

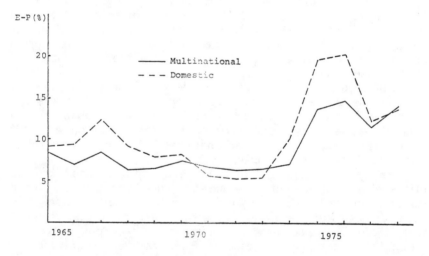

During 1976, despite good expectations, earnings did not grow as fast as anticipated. This caused an increase in share prices that was unwarranted by the earnings growth rate. The E-Ps of both multinationals and domestics declined, but that of the latter did so more rapidly.

In 1977, prices went up but earnings, especially multinational ones, increased even faster. While both multinational and domestic E-Ps rose, the latter did so more mildly probably because of improvements in the U.S. market.

CHEMICAL AND ALLIED PRODUCTS

Chemical shares were expected to perform better than the average of all shares during 1965. While net income and sales were expected to grow by 4 percent, dividends were anticipated to rise by 7 percent. Also, the new tax law was favorable to the industry. The increase in earnings was accompanied by an almost equal increase in prices. The E-Ps for both multinationals and domestics remained relatively stable.

In 1966, while short-term prospects were good, there was a concern that the general business climate could deteriorate in the United States. While the multinational E-Ps remained relatively stable during the year, domestic ones rose moderately.

The domestic earnings fell during 1967. However, this was not accompanied by a similar decrease in prices because investors believed this was temporary and saw better prospects for the longer term. While the E-Ps of the multinationals remained quite stable, those of the domestics fell moderately.

The same situation basically continued in 1968. New facilities and expansions in the United States reduced domestic earnings in the short term but offered good long-term prospects. Chemical sales were expected to grow at par with the United States' GNP during 1968. Multinational E-Ps declined very slightly, while domestic ones fell considerably.

The fact that the long-awaited great increases in earnings did not materialize brought gloom to investors, who became disenchanted with domestic chemical stocks in 1969. The point should be made that chemical stocks, until late 1966, carried unrealistically low E-Ps, which was a holdover from an earlier era when the novelty of chemical technology allowed high growth records. By 1969, these previously "new" products had already become low profit-margin commodities. Yet, there was the general belief that there were still opportunities for new discoveries and hence new products in 1969. During the year, domestic E-Ps rose quite rapidly, while multinational ones remained rather stable most probably because of the better opportunities overseas.

Earnings declines steepened by late 1969 and early 1970 mainly due to cutbacks in automobile production in the United States. However, prices did not decline accordingly because investors thought there would be an upturn by the end of the year. While the multinational E-Ps remained relatively stable, the domestic ones declined considerably.

Although profits began to increase in 1971, this was not reflected in prices due to the hangover from the previous year. Overseas markets were turning more intensely competitive with lower growth rates and profits squeezes. While the domestic E-Ps rose slightly, the multinational ones remained stable.

Sharp earnings gains were expected for 1972. The revaluation of major currencies in 1971 against the dollar gave a competitive edge to U.S. producers in world markets. However, investors felt that this might be of short duration. While multinational E-Ps remained stable, the domestic ones rose moderately.

In 1973, the increase in share prices was not as high as that of earnings due to the overcaution of investors vis-a-vis chemical shares. Both multinational and domestic E-Ps rose rapidly during the year.

FIGURE 7.4. Earnings-Price Ratios – Chemical and Allied Products

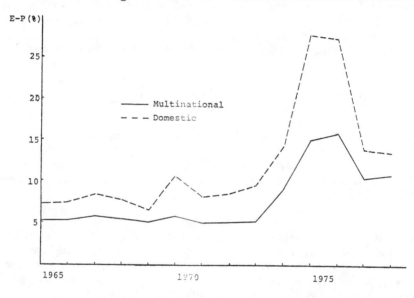

During 1974, chemical stock prices were negatively influenced by the Arab oil embargo despite the fact that earnings increased rapidly. Investors were more wary of domestic shares because of the misperception that the United States would suffer the most from the 1974 recession. While multinational E-Ps rose rapidly, the domestic ones rose far more rapidly.

Recovery began in 1975. While the multinational E-Ps increased only slightly, the domestic ones declined moderately.

In 1976, the U.S. and Western European average expected GNP growth rates were respectively put at 5 and 3 percent. As expected, chemical firms did much better. Although earnings increased, prices increased even faster. While the multinational E-Ps declined rapidly, the domestic ones fell even more rapidly due in part to increased exports from the United States.

During 1977, the fast increase in earnings slowed down, and the weakening of many foreign currencies vis-a-vis the dollar influenced the multinationals negatively. While the multinational E-Ps rose slightly, the domestic ones fell quite moderately.

FABRICATED METAL PRODUCTS

At the beginning of 1965, the two fabricated metal-producing multinational firms in our sample were poorly rated by Value Line. During the year, however, prices did not fall as fast as earnings did, and the multinational E-Ps actually fell. The domestic firms showed little change in any respect, and their E-Ps remained stable.

As far as the U.S. domestic market was concerned, metal containers proved to be quite immune to the 1966 recession. However, the recession adversely affected construction activities, and one of the multinationals was especially affected since it was heavily involved in fabricated metal products used in construction. Thus, despite no apparent changes in foreign markets, the E-Ps of multinationals rose, probably because of the lull in construction.

Both construction and packaging looked promising in 1967. Moreover, the introduction of the new tin-free steel metal containers brightened the prospects for metal fabricators. E-Ps generally declined.

In 1968, packaging became very profitable. Earnings prospects were especially good in metal cans. There were no noteworthy changes in foreign markets. Multinational as well as domestic E-Ps continued their downward slide.

During 1969, prices did not rise as fast as the very rapidly rising earnings in metal containers. One of the multinationals had poor prospects in toiletries both in the United States and abroad. E-Ps of both multinationals and domestics rose, but the former's rise was faster probably due to the problems encountered by that multinational.

While the 1970 prospects were lukewarm for toiletries, they seemed bright for other metal-fabricating activities, partly because of a construction recovery in the United States. As both E-Ps fell, the domestic E-Ps fell even faster.

In 1971, metal packaging was understood to be source of pollution. This increased popular reaction against it and tended to restrict its use in the United States. Construction did not do as well as was previously expected. The performance of toiletries, also, was mediocre in the United States. While multinational E-Ps were stable, the domestic ones rose.

During 1972, toiletries did badly overseas, especially in Western Europe where economic conditions were sluggish. While construction was good in the first half of the year, it began to taper off during the second half. Although 1972 was a difficult year for containers, more distant future prospects looked brighter. Yet, metal-fabricating earnings increased overall. Multinational and domestic E-Ps rose in 1972.

The energy crisis of 1973 affected all aspects of metal fabricating. The construction activities in the United States and Canada were weak. One of the two multinationals did badly in general. Although the other one managed to increase its earnings, this did not seem to influence investors and its share price fell. In the end, the multinational E-Ps rose even faster than the domestic ones, which also rose steeply.

FIGURE 7.5. Earnings-Price Ratios – Fabricated Metal Products

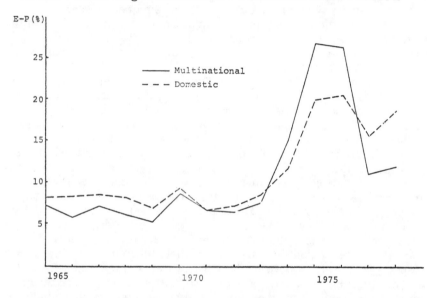

In 1974, earnings prospects for metal-fabricating industries worsened. Higher raw material costs abroad made it even more difficult for multinationals. Share prices fell very sharply and E-Ps for domestics and multinationals continued to rise fast.

In 1975, though there were general improvements both in the United States and abroad, it was the U.S. boom in housing and an upsurge in packaging activities that led the way. Thus, it is rather unlikely that the faster decline in multinational E-Ps as compared to domestic ones was mainly the result of foreign sales.

During 1976, both multinationals had earnings declines far greater than their respective share price declines. Domestic firms did well especially in packaging and construction. Multinational E-Ps declined faster than their domestic counterparts in 1976.

In 1977, there was a marked slowdown in U.S. construction activities. Other conditions seemed to have relatively stabilized. Thus, domestic E-Ps rose substantially faster than the multinational ones.

NONFERROUS METALS

During 1965, prospects for multinationals looked better, not because of better foreign market conditions, but because the two multinationals in our sample dealt heavily with lead and zinc, which had excellent earnings records and prospects. The E-Ps of multinationals declined, while those of the domestics rose.

As lead and zinc became somewhat less attractive during 1966, aluminum and copper, sold mainly by the domestic firms in our sample, came to the limelight because of higher demand from the military, construction, and packaging industries.

In 1967, the greater fall in multinational E-Ps could be partly attributed to the copper strike of U.S. producers. The multinationals in our sample were heavily involved with copper. Moreover, the earnings of multinationals fell because of devaluations in Chile, Zambia, Peru, and the Congo, but shares did not decline accordingly. In the end, while domestic E-Ps declined moderately, multinational E-Ps fell sharply.

The copper strike ended in 1968, but it resulted in an increase of 5 percent in copper prices. Inflation and declining reserves in the United States made gold more attractive. One of the multinationals was heavily involved in lead and zinc, which became attractive for investors. The multinational E-Ps fell faster than the domestic ones did in 1968.

During 1969, prospects for lead and zinc became dimmer, while those of copper greatly improved. Gold was losing its attractiveness. Although the earnings of aluminum increased, fears of recession in the United States led to a fall in the corresponding share prices. The multinational E-Ps rose even faster than the domestic ones.

Despite a dim beginning, 1970 proved to be a good year for metals in general. A resurgence in the U.S. and world economies was expected. Metal share prices went up, and the E-Ps of both multinationals and domestics went down.

During 1971, lead and zinc had better prospects than other metals, and the share price of one of the multinationals dealing with these metals rose. A countering but lesser influence was the appreciation of European and Japanese currencies in relation to the U.S. dollar. During the year, while multinational E-Ps remained stable, the domestic E-Ps rose.

In 1972, the earnings of domestic companies that dealt with gold rose but without a corresponding increase in share prices because of uncertainties in the U.S. economy. The domestic E-Ps rose substantially faster than the multinational ones.

In 1973, there were major upheavals and uncertainties arising from the war in the Middle East and the energy crisis. The prices of the majority of metal shares, like others, dropped sharply. Metals that did well were gold and silver as well as lead, which seemed to have good prospects as an additive to gasoline, thus increasing fuel efficiency. Lead could also be used in battery production. The E-Ps of domestics rose somewhat faster than those of multinationals during the year. In any case, both rose very rapidly.

FIGURE 7.6. Earnings-Price Ratios – Nonferrous Metals

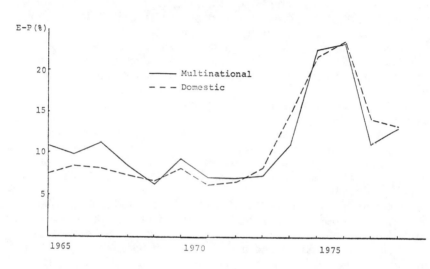

An examination of the two multinationals in our sample shows that their earnings rose tremendously during 1974. However, there were no reflections of this on share prices because of uncertainties primarily in the rest of the world and secondarily in the United States. The domestics underwent the same phenomenon though somewhat more moderately. The E-Ps continued their rapid rise in 1974 with the multinational E-Ps rising even faster than those of the domestic firms abroad, which were able to export more.

During 1975, the slowdown in the increase of earnings was not accompanied by a drop in share prices. Prospects were moderate in general but were better for lead and zinc. Both multinational and domestic E-Ps rose, but the latter rose faster. This was probably because of investors' perception that the worst was over in the world's economic uncertainties.

In 1976, while prices went up, earnings fell. Of the metals, lead did extremely well especially in the second half of the year. Multinational and domestic E-Ps both fell rapidly; the former declined even more drastically.

While prospects for aluminum looked dim, they were better for gold and copper at the beginning of 1977. At the end of the year, however, there was a complete reversal of the situation, and this influenced the multinationals negatively. While domestic E-Ps fell, multinational ones rose.

FOOD PRODUCTS

Despite increasing competition both in the United States and abroad, some of the food companies in our sample introduced new products in the domestic market in 1965. Still, the expected increase in sales and net income for the food companies was better than the average of all companies. During 1965, the multinational E-Ps rose moderately, while the domestic ones remained stable.

In 1966, food companies were squeezed between higher ingredient costs, resulting from higher food demand, and attempts at keeping price hikes at a minimum. Thus, there was a heavy pressure on profit margins. However, a high demand for food products prevented substantial declines in share prices. During the year, both domestic and multinational E-Ps rose only slightly.

Investors' perception of food as having a relatively inelastic demand in the long run as well as increasing product prices countered the slight fall in demand at the end of 1967 and the beginning of 1968. The three multinationals in our sample were traditionally more unwilling to boost prices and were thus more prone to price-cost squeezes. During 1967, while the domestic E-Ps fell slightly, the multinational ones rose moderately.

There were mixed trends in 1968. At the beginning, there was a price-cost squeeze, which reduced the earnings. Later in the year, however, a redressment of earnings took place, and an increase in earnings of at least 7 percent was expected for 1969. The three multinationals in our sample finally increased their product prices after a time lag. Also, their foreign operations were very profitable. While both domestic and multinational E-Ps fell, the latter did so faster.

In 1969, the earnings of the multinationals increased faster than their stock prices, thus resulting in an increase for E-Ps that was moderate probably because of the countereffect of high demand for food. The domestic E-Ps remained stable.

During 1970, the multinationals in our sample performed very well both in the United States and abroad. Their stock prices increased even faster than the earnings, thus leading to lower multinational E-Ps. The domestic E-Ps remained stable during the year.

Because of the relative immunity of food demand to an economic slump, food shares did better than others during 1971. However, investors who expected a recovery in the U.S. economy were more tempted by the undervalued shares in other industries. During 1971, the E-Ps of both multinationals and domestics rose moderately.

In 1972, because of the increasing trend and demand for ready-to-eat food outside the United States, foreign earnings of multinationals continued their upward trend. However, these increased earnings had little reflection on multinational share prices because investors continued to be interested in the undervalued stocks of other industries. During the year, the multinational E-Ps rose faster than the domestic ones.

FIGURE 7.7. Earnings-Price Ratios – Food Products

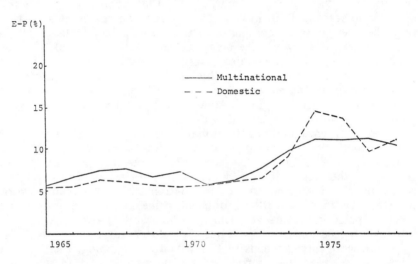

In 1973, price regulations in the United States influenced the domestics more than the multinationals. Stock price declines were greater for the domestics, even though earnings went up for both. Domestic E-Ps rose faster than multinational ones did.

During 1974, domestic food demand did not fall despite the recession. However, the continuing price freeze discouraged investments in domestic food shares. Multinationals were more immune to the freeze. In 1974, domestic E-Ps rose faster than multinational ones.

In 1975, while demand persisted, the price of ingredients in the United States plummeted, interest rates came down, and packaging costs levelled off. There was a considerable increase in sales and profits in the domestic market. Foreign markets were not so active. During the year, domestic E-Ps fell while multinational ones remained stable.

During 1976, further declines in U.S. costs, especially the price of ingredients, made domestic food shares very attractive to investors. Despite increasing earnings, prices rose even faster. While multinational E-Ps were stable, domestic ones fell considerably.

In 1977, good trends continued for food but, with the U.S. economy pulling out of recession, investors began to look at undervalued shares of other industries. Foreign food prospects looked even better. While the multinational E-Ps fell, the domestic E-Ps rose because investors did not respond to earnings increases.

After having examined the events that may possibly have influenced the earnings-price ratios, it would now be appropriate to take note of some noteworthy results.

The earnings-price ratios are influenced not only by multinationality versus domesticity per se but also by other factors like demand for various products within a certain industry group, the performance of a single company when the sample is small, government interventions like price fixings and tariffs, shortages or gluts of raw materials, exchange rates, the marketing of new products in the United States and their possible eventual adoptions abroad, the level of worldwide competition for various products, and finally the location of raw materials. The last factor explains, to an important degree, why petroleum refining and food products run contrary to the hypothesis of this study. If the multinationals are heavily dependent on raw material located outside the United States, they will be more subject to pressures by host countries and less indispensable, since they have less leverage than other industries that depend far more on high technology. As for fabricated metals, the erratic performance of one of the two multinationals seems to influence the results significantly. This firm is rather heavily involved in toiletries, which have not been doing so well during a major part of the period under study. Of these two factors, the location of raw materials outside the United States is one which has a long-term, if not lasting, influence on the comparative risk of multinationals and domestics. All the other factors can work both ways at one time or another and thus, in conformity with the law of large numbers, they would tend to cancel one another. In fact, this is a major reason for our taking a relatively long period of time and sampling several industries, each with a number of firms.

The same law of large numbers helps one to find rather related results in the long term for the cost of equity capital (k_e) and earnings-price ratios. The same is not true for the short term because there are simply not enough years to make the law of large numbers work. Again, this shows that the additional labor involved in studying a long-term period was worth it.

8

Forward-Looking and Historical Growth Rates

While the main purpose of this study is to explore the relative changes in multinational and domestic costs of equity capital, the data set also lends itself to making some useful comments about the controversy over the use of forward-looking estimates of growth versus estimates based on historical data when incorporating a growth element into the cost of equity capital calculations.

Researchers agree that one of the most, if not the most, difficult problems encountered in calculating the cost of equity capital is the derivation of a good estimate of the growth rate. In the past, most analysts have used historical holding period return spreads for their calculations. R. G. Ibbotson and R. A. Sinquefield (1976a; 1976b), in a series of studies, presented year-by-year historical rates of return for different asset classes and showed how to use the historical data in simulating future return distributions.

If a company has experienced a relatively steady growth in earnings and dividends and if this rate of growth is expected to continue in the future, then past growth rate might be used for projecting future growth. However, there are certain problems with historical rates involving methods of calculation, holding periods, and conceptual matters.

First, according to Fisher and Lorie (1966, pp. 162-69), alternative ways of calculating procedures cause substantial differences in reported rates of return on portfolios. The choice of stocks included in the stock portfolio, determination of different weights to each security, and if necessary handling taxes, brokerage commissions, capital gains taxes, etc. can exert a substantial influence on estimating the cost of equity capital.

The length of the holding period used in calculations can result in a great difference in the final outcome. Short holding periods will cause very volatile returns. The calculated rate of return on common stocks (before personal taxes) ranged from 8.1 to 13.4 percent even with holding periods ranging 25 to 50 years (Brigham and Shome 1979). Also, the choice of an ending point would have a tremendous effect on the calculated returns if, during a year, the stock market closed very strongly or very weakly.

There is also a conceptual weakness in using past data to estimate returns on equity. It is generally accepted that investors are interested in the anticipated returns of a portfolio, not the realized (past) returns.

If market earnings expectations are rational, then they should be measured by the best available return forecasts. Brown and Rozeff (1978), under the rational expectations hypothesis, tested the widely used forward-looking Value Line Investment Survey forecasts against historical studies, using nonparametric statistics. They concluded that direct measures of earnings expectations, such as security analysts' forecasts, were superior to time series forecasts, which neglect potentially useful information. Sharpe (1978, pp. 343-45) also indicates that the Value Line Investment Survey's ranking of expected stock performance "beats the market" by about 10 percent a year. Each week, every one of about 1,600 stocks is assigned one of five ranks (highest to lowest). While the top-ranked stocks "beat the market" by about 10 percent per year, the bottom-ranked ones were "beaten by the market" by 10 percent.

Generally, the ex post realized return is quite different from the ex ante expected return. It is sometimes argued that investors, over a long period, actually earn returns that are equal to their required returns (Brigham and Shome 1979, pp. 12-13). Supposedly, if investors are disappointed by low returns over some period, then the security prices will decrease to the point where returns in subsequent periods will pull the average realized return back up to the expected level. However, there is no evidence supporting this argument.

Some analysts argue that investors, when making capital budgeting, have a good idea of expected and required returns and use this knowledge when setting the rates. If a reasonable degree of proficiency is assumed in the capital-budgeting process, then, ex post returns will turn out to be close to ex ante returns. However, this proposition assumes that companies already know, with a fair degree of precision, the cost of equity capital.

These problems, together with other economic difficulties, like inflation, make the estimation of returns based on historical data highly questionable. Analysts have argued that it is not generally satisfactory to use only past trends for purposes of estimating the cost of capital and have developed other methods for making growth forecasts.

Brigham and Shome (1979, pp. 21-27) used one of the widely employed procedures for forecasting long-term future growth rates in their study of estimating a market risk premium. Their method involves multiplying the fraction of a company's earnings that investors expect to retain (b) by the expected rate of return on book equity (ROE): g = b x ROE.

In order to get exactly correct estimates of future growth, the percentage of earnings retained and the expected future rate of return on book equity should be measured accurately and stay constant over time. Furthermore, the company is assumed to sell no new common stock or to sell it at book value. Brigham and Shome argue that these three conditions are expected to hold true into the indefinite future and that the formula gives a reasonably accurate estimate of long-term growth. One of their propositions is that most of the companies have reasonably stable target payout ratios over time; so their target retention rates (b) are reasonably stable. Variations in retention rates will be around the target values. Therefore, they take an average of retention rates in the recent past to estimate b. They examine two alternative methods for estimating growth rates.

In their first method, which assumes that investors give a greater weight to more recent data than to earlier data, they calculate b and ROE as the weighted averages of the expected retention rates and returns on book equity in the market. In the second method, they assume that investors expect retention rates, as a matter of corporate policy, either to be stable or fluctuating around a target level. Then, they calculate the expected retention rate for the market as the ratio of total earnings retained to total earnings available over the preceding five years. For the market ROE, they use the notion that dividends are paid out of "normalized" earnings. Hence dividends can be used to estimate normalized ROE.* They determine the normalized rate of return on book equity for the market from the normalized data of individual companies.

---

*The normalized rate of return on average book equity is defined as:

$$\text{Normalized ROE}_i = \frac{\text{Expected Earnings}}{\text{Expected Book Value}}$$

$$= \frac{\text{Expected Dividends}}{\text{Expected Payout Rate}} \times \frac{1}{\text{Expected Book Value}}$$

$$= \frac{\text{Current Dividends } (1 + g)}{(\text{Expected Payout}) \ (\text{Current Book Value}) \ (1 + g)}$$

$$= \frac{\text{Current Dividends}}{(1 - \text{Expected Retention Rate}) \ (\text{Current Book Value})}$$

Although their most critical assumptions about the constant growth Gordon model, retention rate, and returns on book equity over the last four or five years seem reasonable, they maintain the impossibility of ascertaining the "true" aggregate expected growth rate.

In an earlier study, Malkiel (1979) based his growth rate on Value Line earnings growth forecasts. Further, he assumed that all growth rates are expected to decline exponentially to the long-term national growth rate (currently 3.6 percent) after the initial five-year period. Using the Gordon model to estimate the expected rate of return on the 30 Dow Jones Industrial stocks each year from 1960 to 1977, he performed a number of calculations with different horizon periods before the growth rate fell to its "permanent" level. The results of these calculations were remarkably robust, and the estimated risk premiums are very similar to those of the infinite horizon model.

In this study, the cost of equity capital is calculated in two ways, using historical and forward-looking growth rates from the Value Line Investment Survey.

In order to make the comparison more meaningful, we use a cost of equity capital with historical growth different from that of the Kohers method, which was explained in Chapter 3. The present method uses the same Value Line dividend yield (D/P) as that used in our cost of equity capital calculations with forward-looking growth. It will be remembered that we calculated a different (quarterly) dividend yield for the Kohers method. The historical growth rates in the present method were taken from Value Line, which took the average growth rate for each five-year period immediately preceding the year for which the cost of equity capital was calculated. For instance, the Value Line of 1965 indicates what the average growth rates has been for 1960-65. Likewise, one can look at the Value Line of 1974 to find the average growth rate for 1969-74. Thus, it is assumed that the average growth for the past five years will continue in the future.

As already mentioned, Brown and Rozeff (1978) and Sharpe (1978) show that Value Line data are used by a great number of investors, and the predictions are proven to be superior to some other models (like the Box and Jenkins Time Series Forecasting, which is accepted as being a relatively sophisticated time series model). One of the test results attributes Value Line's superiority to its use of the information set available to it on the quarterly earnings announcement date and not to the acquisition of information arising after the quarterly earnings announcement date. Early acquisition of this incremental information has a positive effect on predicting the next quarter's earnings.

The results of these two methods with growth rates based on historical and forward-looking data are shown in Figures 8.1 and 8.2.

Two significant differences can be observed right away. First, for the same years, k_e based on past data shows greater fluctuations than k_e based on anticipated data. This is probably the result of security analysts' assessments of the erratic periods. This is to say, k_e based on anticipated data could reflect analysts' corrective judgments for the abnormal deviations, while k_e based on past data would carry the abnormal deviations over.

The second noticeable difference is that k_e based on past data follows k_e based on anticipated data with a one-year lag in many cases. One could perhaps say that the analysts might anticipate the effects of various factors that influence the market earlier than these factors show their effect on the market. Therefore, k_e based on past data might lag behind k_e based on anticipated data, since past data might reflect that information only after a certain time.

FIGURE 8.1. k_e with Forward-looking Growth vs. k_e with Historical Growth (multinational firms)

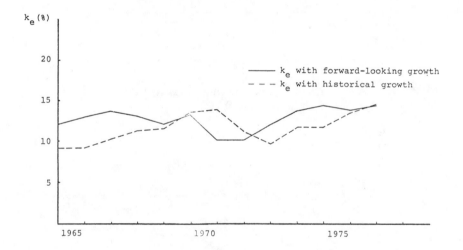

When we compare our results with those of Brigham and Shome (1979), we see that our multinational and domestic data follow those of Brigham and Shome quite well but at a somewhat higher level. The difference is probably the result of the different samples used in the studies. The cash-flow earnings growth, which is used in our calculations, may also have contributed to this difference. On the average, the cash-flow earnings growth is somewhat higher than growth based on the expected rate of return on book equity, which is used by Brigham and Shome.

For a comparison, we show the cost of equity capital calculated by Brigham and Shome (1979, p. 31) together with our forward-looking multinational k_e and domestic k_e on Figures 8.3 and 8.4.

FIGURE 8.2. k_e with Forward-looking Growth vs. k_e with Historical Growth (domestic firms)

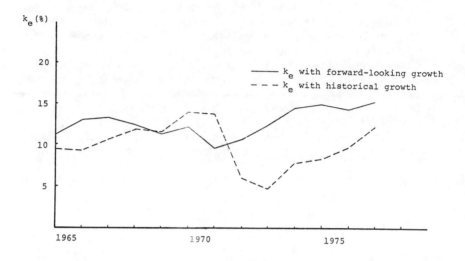

FIGURE 8.3. k_e with Forward-looking Growth (multinational firms) vs. k_e by Brigham and Shome (S&P 400 industrial firms)

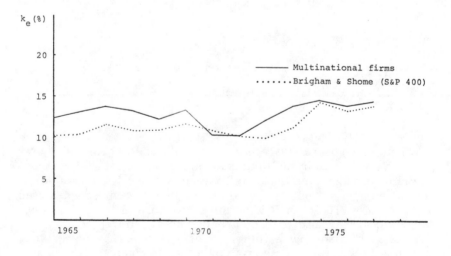

FIGURE 8.4. k_e with Forward-looking Growth (domestic firms) vs. k_e by Brigham and Shome (S&P 400 industrial firms)

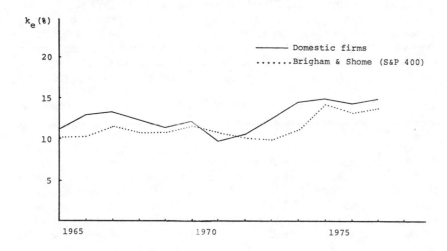

An interesting situation emerges from the comparison of our forward-looking k_es with our historical k_es and with the k_es of Brigham and Shome. Despite the use of a different sample, our k_es with forward-looking growth rates follow the Brigham and Shome k_es more closely than they do our k_es with historical growth rates. This shows that growth rates can have an important effect on the cost of equity capital. In this case, the difference of growth rates was more important than the difference of samples.

The results of our calculations seem to follow the economic events of the period relatively well. As explained in the appendix, the inflationary bout beginning with the U.S. military intervention in Vietnam in 1965 had pulled the stock prices down contrary to the previous inflationary rounds. According to Sobel (1975, p. 288), the Dow Jones Industrial Average was at 874.13 at the end of 1964. As inflation began to accelerate, stock prices began to fall. As a result, the cost of equity capital increased as seen in Figures 8.1 and 8.2. While the decline in stock prices reached a minimum at the end of 1966, k_e in our figures reached a peak. Although the sluggish economic conditions persisted in the beginning of 1967, the monetary authorities' more expansionary policy made the interest rates decrease. Business fixed investment kept increasing, and stock prices picked up some gains at the end of the year. While slow economic expansion continued in 1968, Sobel (1975, p. 320) writes that the Dow Jones rose above the 950 mark and reached its peak in December when our k_e went down. After this peak, stock prices began to fall until the middle of 1970, apparently affecting k_e reversely.

In the second half of 1970, stock prices recovered and, in December, the Dow Jones exceeded the 800 mark. Total GNP, which had fallen 0.4 percent in 1970, began to rise slowly, and its growth rate was calculated as 2.7 percent for the whole of 1971 (Economist Quarterly* 1972a). There was a corresponding decrease in our k_e figures. Inflationary forces remained strong during the year. In August 1971, President Nixon announced 90-day wage and price controls to curb inflation. Although stock prices continued to increase and corporate profits recovered, the high inflation rate and large relative price changes created uncertainties for long-run future planning. Probably, businessmen's fear of price controls that would impinge on corporate profitability was the cause of the k_e increases in 1972, as shown in the figures.

Rising interest rates were accompanied by substantial inflation in 1973. In October, the Arab oil boycott worsened the situation. Although corporate profits continued to be good in 1973, several speculative shares lost value, and that increased the worries about the overall economy (Sobel 1975, p. 363). In 1974, impeachment debates and Nixon's resignation added to the uncertainties, and the economy began to decline. By early 1975, it was believed that the economy had entered its worst recession since the 1930s. All these events showed their reflections on stock prices. The Dow Jones fell in 1973 and 1974 sharply. In our figures, k_e continued to increase during these periods.

At the beginning of 1975, the gloomy outlook of the economy continued to prevail. Real decrease in the GNP, during the first quarter of 1975, was 11.3 percent. Industrial production was down 12.4 percent in April compared to the same period of the previous year, whereas consumer prices were up 10.2 percent (Economist Quarterly, 1975b). The economy started to recover in the second half of 1975. The real GNP growth reached a 13.2 percent annual rate in the third quarter due to the rapid increase in spending on cars (Economist Quarterly, 1975c). The fall in some food prices brought about a moderation to the increase of wholesale prices. While the stock market was recovering, expectations were higher for 1976. The cost of equity capital continued to increase, though at a lower rate, in 1975. The rate of increase was even lower for the domestic firms.

The recovery that started in the second half of 1975 went on to the last quarter of 1976. Industrial production was growing, while profits and share prices continued to go up steadily. The Dow Jones Industrial Average was 947.92 for the year (Economic Indicators 1979, p. 31). As a result, there was a decrease in k_e as shown in the figures.

---

*The Economist Intelligence Unit Quarterly Economic Review: U.S.A. is referred to as Economist Quarterly.

During the first quarter of 1977, pessimism about inflation and fear of price controls were dominating Wall Street. Although GNP was expected to rise by 5 percent, stockholding was reduced because of policy uncertainties. Wholesale prices and interest rates were increasing in the second half of 1977. The Dow Jones Industrial Average fell to 894.63 and continued to fall in 1978 (Economic Indicators 1979, p. 31). The cost of equity capital started to rise again in 1976 and 1977.

This chapter has shown that the type of growth rate used in calculating the cost of equity capital is quite important. We have found that forward-looking (ex ante) growth rates yield results that are very different from those given by historical (ex post) growth rates. Just as Malkiel (1979) and Brigham and Shome (1979) have argued, we have maintained that forward-looking growth rates reflect investors' attitudes better than historical ones do.

9

The Field of
International Business

GENERAL BACKGROUND

The purpose of explaining the field of international business and its evolution is to see what the existing theories are, whether they help to explain our findings, and whether our findings corroborate or disprove them entirely or partially.

International business was once thought to be synonymous with international trade — the importing and exporting of goods among nations of the world. However, with the proliferation of direct investment, this narrow definition of international business (management) is no longer sufficient. Before going straight into theories dealing with the direct investments of multinational firms, it would be appropriate to mention briefly a paradigmatic theory of comparative advantage, which has been a stimulator of later theories.

The theory of comparative advantage as expounded by Ricardo, John Stuart Mill, and other followers of Adam Smith can be expressed in the following manner:

1. Whether or not one of two regions is absolutely more efficient in the production of every good than is the other, if each specializes in the products in which it has a comparative advantage (greatest relative efficiency), trade will be mutually profitable to both regions. Real wages of productive factors will rise in both places.

2. An ill-designed prohibitive tariff, far from helping the protected factor of production, will instead reduce its real

wage by making imports expensive and by making the whole world less productive through eliminating the efficiency inherent in the best pattern of specialization and division of labor (Vernon 1971, p. 107).

Ricardo measured all costs in terms of labor. Modern day economists like Ohlin propound that the theory is still valid, even if a labor theory of value is not assumed. Again, Ohlin stated that free movements of labor and capital between countries would tend to equalize wages and factor prices (Vernon 1971, p. 666).

First of all, Ricardo's idea is firmly based upon the "laissez faire, laisser passer" doctrine of Adam Smith, of whom he is a follower. The law of comparative advantage clearly assumes a liberal free economy with minimum government interference.

The general theory of international capital flows deals with movements of capital from one country to another in response to differences in the marginal productivity of capital. This means that capital will go to places where the rate of return or yield is higher, assuming the risk is the same. However, this theory has been unable to explain a great part of the sizable flows of direct investment capital in recent years. For instance, U.S. firms are making large direct investments in Europe, while European firms are simultaneously making sizable direct investments in the United States. In addition to that, direct overseas investments do not necessarily involve capital transfers from one country to another since the investing firms may simply borrow funds in the host country. Hence, new explanations for the reasons motivating multinational firms to invest abroad are needed. The microtheory of the firm has later been integrated with the macrotheory of international capital movements. This has produced a series of theories like the "defensive investment" concept of Lamfalussy (1961), which states that direct investment is undertaken where there are large and growing markets in view of long-term rather than short-term profitability. Our empirical test yields results that seem to support partially Lamfalussy's concept in our sample. Thus, the average cost of equity capital of all multinationals declines in relation to that of the domestics. This shows that these initially "unattractive looking" investments were made in anticipation of better performance in the future. Another example is Aliber's theory, which explains overseas direct investment as a currency phenomenon brought about by the market's preference for holding assets denominated in selected currencies, which are, of course, strong currencies (Aliber 1970, p. 34). Both these theories remain unsatisfactory in explaining the reasons for direct investment. In fact, the development of a theoretical framework for explaining international business patterns has been outrun by the practice of international business. The new and more complex patterns of international business cannot be satisfactorily explained by traditional economic theories of international trade and investment.

However, new approaches inspired by the facts of international business are beginning to provide a theoretical framework. The main ones are (a) the oligopoly model; (b) the product cycle model; (c) the international transmission of resources; and (d) the portfolio theory.

The above theories combine the business and economics approach. We can thus see what the main models are, in what respects they are adequate or inadequate, how each of them fits into the whole field, and how they are evolving.

We may now take a look at each of these theories separately.

MAIN THEORIES

The Oligopoly Model

According to the oligopoly model, the firm makes foreign direct investments to benefit from a certain quasi-monopoly advantage it has. The advantage of the multinational firm over local firms may be due to (a) technology; (b) access to capital; (c) differentiated products built on advertising; (d) better management; or (e) economies of scale.

A cost-benefit analysis must indicate whether that special advantage overweighs the disadvantage of operating in a foreign environment. According to Caves (1969, p. 5), a cost-benefit analysis must also be made to determine whether this advantage is important enough to more than offset other ways of exploiting rent such as licensing or exporting. This comes close to Lamfalussy's "defensive investment" concept, which was explained before.

The oligopoly model not only explains "horizontal investments" for foreign production of goods and services similar to those products in the domestic market but also explains "vertical investments" to produce overseas a raw or intermediary input for the domestic production process. This latter investment may raise barriers to the entry of a new competitor and protect their oligopoly position.

Although the oligopoly model combines to a certain extent the fields of economics and business management, it still cannot answer some important phenomena. For instance, why did firms not take advantage of their quasi-monopoly positions to such an extent before? Moreover, this model can explain continued rapid expansion in foreign investment only to the extent that the special advantages of the investing firms are expanding (Cooper 1968, p. 89). Another limitation of the theory is that it is not integrated with alternative ways such as exports or licensing. Also, it does not sufficiently explain acquisitions and mergers (Aliber 1970, p. 20).

After this succinct explanation of the theory, it would be appropriate to show how it relates to our findings. It must be stressed that the above-mentioned five advantages of the multinational firms are over local firms in host countries and not necessarily over U.S. domestic firms. So this aspect has only limited relevance as far as our study is concerned. At best, it can give a partial explanation of why the firms in our sample have gone multinational. The same can be said for the "horizontal investments" and "vertical investments". On the other hand, the findings of this study can explain a substantial part of what was left unexplained by the oligopoly model, namely, the reason for the continued rapid expansion of multinationals during the last decade or two. The maturing of both the host countries and the multinational firms as well as the improvement of communications, as shown before, are new dimensions that further clarify the process of multinationalization. If the scope of the oligopoly model were sufficiently widened to incorporate our findings, the new synthesis could certainly be more functional than the present model.

The Product Cycle Theory

According to the product cycle theory, direct foreign investment is a natural stage in the life cycle of a new product from its birth to its maturity and eventual decline. This model, which has significantly contributed to a better understanding of the evolution of multinational firms, is associated with the work of Raymond Vernon (1966). Accordingly, large firms have a technological advantage due to their capacity to carry out intensive and costly research and development activities. As a result, they discover technologically advanced, or at least differentiable, products. These products are introduced in the home country markets and, after a certain time, are exported. As the new products reach maturity, competition from quite similar products decreases the profit margins. At this stage, manufacturing locations abroad are used in order to lower production costs and thereby to be able to compete in the host country and possibly other country markets. We must, however, mention the point that after the new product stage, there are two additional stages: the mature product stage and the standardized product stage. In the mature product stage, as technology becomes sufficiently routine to be transferred to a firm's firm, export chances decrease, and as foreign demand increases to the point that it is worthwhile to establish a production facility of economic size, the enterprise is induced to produce abroad, generally in other developed countries. Then, in the standardized product stage, production may shift to low-cost locations in the less developed countries from which goods may be exported back to the home country and other markets.

The product cycle model has been able to explain the past performance of certain multinational manufacturing firms. Also, several empirical studies have supported this theory by showing a correlation between industries (and companies) with intensive research and development activities and direct foreign investment (Gruber, Mehta, and Vernon 1967; Baldwin, 1971).

Our selections of a sample of multinational corporations and domestic corporations from the Fortune list of the 500 largest corporations in the United States partially supports Vernon's theory. Whereas Kohers (1971, pp. 65-66) identified 55 U.S. multinational and 65 U.S. domestic corporations for his sample, we found only 28 multinationals and 28 domestics during the 1965-78 period. The decrease in the number of eligible firms was a result of the increasing multinationalization of U.S. firms. Thus, many of the firms that were domestics in 1965 became multinationals during the 1970s. Another relevant aspect of the results of our study deals with the trends of petroleum and food products. The former and, to a lesser extent, the latter are dependent on scarce raw materials needed by the parent firm in the United States. Petroleum products run contrary to our hypothesis according to the trend test for earnings-price ratios, while the same phenomenon is true for food products when dealing with the cost of equity capital. As previously mentioned, the rest of the groups are primarily supporting our hypothesis or, to a lesser degree, are insignificant. Thus, those groups that have technologically more advanced products seem to support the product cycle theory, since the earnings-price ratio and cost of equity capital trends for multinationals are declining in relation to domestics. This apparent reduction in risk is apparently due to the need that host countries feel for the technologically advanced product. This is not valid for technologically less sophisticated and/or raw-material-oriented industry groups.

The product cycle theory does not really explain foreign investments in scarce raw materials needed by the parent firm in the home country, that is, in mining, oil, and plantation operations. Vernon himself says that the theory does not apply to firms that have been international for a long time and acquired a "global habit of mind" (Vernon 1971, p. 107). Moreover, the model does not emphasize enough location economics. If there is enough demand for the product and if the transportation costs are reduced sufficiently, it would pay to make direct investment abroad. The establishment of automotive industries in several developing countries by multinational corporations attest to this idea. Savings in import tariffs should also be taken into account wherever applicable.

The product cycle model associated with Vernon has been expanded by a number of persons like L. T. Wells, R. B. Stobaugh, H. G. Johnson, W. Gruber, D. Mehta, R. E. Baldwin, and by Vernon himself through his later writings. Our findings, and possibly others to come, indicate that the product cycle theory gives only partial explanations and needs to widen its scope.

The International Transmission of Resources Theory

The international transmission of resources model of Fayerweather (1969, pp. 15-50) is essentially an extension of classical trade theory. It proposes that the multinational firm plays an important role in the transmission of resources like technological, managerial, and entrepreneurial skills, as well as the usual natural resources, capital, and labor. Differentials in the supply-demand relationships of resources among countries generate basic economic pressures for the international flow of resources and create opportunities for the multinational firm. The intervention of the nation-states may reshape these resource-differential relationships, which are essentially determined by free economic forces into the actual patterns of opportunities open to the firm. The firm makes use of these opportunities according to its strategy and characteristics.

It can easily be seen that Fayerweather's theory combines classical trade and investment theory with the behavioral models of the business enterprise. The theory distinguishes the resource transmission role of the multinational firm from that of the purely domestic firm in the following manner: (1) the multinational firm, which has developed a global perspective, looks at resource differentials among countries; and (2) the multinational firm also takes into account the interventions of the nation-states.

Although this model makes a significant contribution to explaining most of the dimensions of international business, it still does not explain the process whereby firms acquire their global perspectives in the beginning. Moreover, it does not try to examine the evolutionary history of multinational firms. As far as our findings are concerned, the transmission of resources model explains, at least to a degree, why petroleum products and food products do not yield the same results as the other groups do. As already mentioned, these two groups are more oriented toward raw materials (natural resources) than the others, which are essentially technologically oriented. Thus, the former groups have to deal with host countries that are in a position of strength because they possess the scarce raw materials. Thus, the multinationals operating under such circumstances may look less secure because of real or imagined reasons. On the other hand, the multinationals belonging to the other industry groups seem to be in a stronger position because the host countries need their advanced technological skills (resources). Thus, the model can give a partial explanation as to why multinationals, compared to domestics, can become riskier, while the opposite is true for the other groups. Although the international transmission of resources theory makes an attempt to introduce behavioral explanations, it does not explain a process whereby both the multinationals and the host countries can adapt to changing environments and different conditions by a learning or cognitive process. If our findings about the maturing of multinationals and host countries were integrated with this model, its comprehension and explanatory power would certainly increase.

Portfolio Theory

Levy and Sarnat (1970) explained that an investor could decrease fluctuations arising from risky investments by holding an internationally diversified portfolio of securities as compared with a domestically diversified portfolio.

The riskiness of an operation can be defined in terms of the likely variability of future returns from the operation (Weston and Brighan 1975, p. 309). The overall risk can be reduced if there is an efficient diversification of investments. In other words, the correlation between or among the investments must be as close to a perfectly negative correlation as possible, or vice versa, as far from a perfectly positive correlation as possible. This idea was formally formulated by Markowitz (1959) and then extended by Sharpe.

The same idea could be applied to an internationally diversified portfolio of securities or direct foreign investments. The Levy-Sarnat model assumes that rates of return on investments are less correlated among countries than they are in any one country. As long as expected rates of return are not perfectly correlated, it is possible to find a portfolio of investments that minimizes risk for a given rate of return. This suggests that multinational firms should sometimes prefer investments with lower returns if the correlation between these returns and the returns from the actual operations are negatively enough correlated.

The Levy-Sarnat model does explain a part of our findings. When the betas (of the capital asset pricing model) of the multinational and domestic firms are compared, one can see that the systematic risk of the multinationals increased in relation to the domestics after 1973, when the economic cycles of the United States and other industrialized countries were almost in unison. Thus, there was virtually no room left for international diversification. This aspect has been explained in greater detail in previous chapters.

We have seen how the Ricardian comparative advantage theory has paved the way for later theories in international economics and business. Weston (1966, pp. 31-35) draws a parallel between classical absolutist (Newtonian) physics and classical economics together with a parallel between relativistic (Einsteinian) physics and the behavioral theory of the firm. In line with the general tendency, one can clearly see a trend toward more relativism or behaviorism in the theories of international business. However, there still is a long way to go before there are theories that give more complete explanations of international business. The above theories and models, which are really the main ones, partially explain our findings and in turn get some empirical support from our findings.

10

Conclusions

SUMMARY AND CONCLUSIONS

The purpose of this study is to test the hypothesis that the cost of equity capital and hence the total risk of U.S. multinational firms would decrease in relation to that of U.S. domestic firms because of the maturing attitudes of both the host countries and the multinational corporations, as well as the improvement of communications.

Before carrying out the test, a study of host countries, which were recipients of U.S. foreign direct investment, was made. It showed that during the period under study, most of these countries had adopted a more mature and sophisticated attitude vis-a-vis the multinational firms. They specified the type of foreign direct investment they sought more clearly and made the rules more specific and clear. Likewise, the multinational firms became more mature, experienced, and sophisticated in their relationships with host countries. Moreover, communications showed major improvements during the period. Thus, it was concluded that conditions became more favorable during the 1970s as opposed to the 1960s.

The results of our empirical test were generally supportive of the hypothesis. It was found that the costs of equity capital and the earnings-price ratios for the overall averages of U.S. multinational firms decreased in relation to those of U.S. domestic firms during the 1965-78 period. This means that the total risk of the multinational firms decreased in relation to that of the domestic firms. Systematic risk, as measured by beta values, was roughly the same for both during the 1971-73 period. After that, the beta average of the domestic firms decreased in relation to that of the multi-nationals because of the synchronism of economic cycles in major Western industrialized countries.

Making use of the test results, we compared the effects of forward-looking growth rates on the cost of equity capital with those of historical growth rates. In our case, it was found that a difference in the method of calculating a growth rate had a greater influence on the cost of equity capital than a difference of samples did. This was an extension of our basic findings.

Finally, the development of the field of international business and its main theories were explained. It was found that, in general, they help to explain our findings, though only partially. Likewise, the findings gave only some partial support to these theories. The implication is that the field of international business needs more comprehensive and complete theories. Again, this was an extension of our study.

SUGGESTIONS FOR ADDITIONAL RESEARCH

The cost of equity capital and other measures of risk for each industry group could be the subject of a major research effort, which would take into account the influence of events specifically affecting that industry. However, due to the lack of published material, such a study would necessitate field studies, interviews, and questionnaire surveys. Both the investors and the persons working in that industry group should be contacted. Naturally, because of the confidentiality of some of the required information, the reticence of at least a part of those interviewed would certainly be a limitation.

In this study, we tried to show the influence of some of the major economic events on the cost of equity capital and other risk measures pertaining to our sample. However, a far more comprehensive multiple regression model with a large number of variables might give more precise results. A well-known example of such a comprehensive study is that of Lawrence Klein and his research team at the University of Pennsylvania. Using hundreds of variables, they use a multiple regression model that makes forecasts of the U.S. economy. Obviously, such a study for multinational corporations would also require large resources.

IMPLICATIONS

The results of this study are of importance for investors, corporate managers, and host countries. A reduction of the cost of equity capital and the total risk has implications for all three. The investor will find that the shares of multinational firms are less risky. The corporate managers will be in a more comfortable position when contemplating foreign direct investment and, because of the risk-return trade-off, will settle for lower returns on a ceteris paribus basis. This situation also favors the host countries, which should normally be able to get foreign direct investment at a lower cost.

Our comparison of forward-looking versus historical growth rates used in calculating the cost equity capital showed that different methods of calculating such a growth rate result in substantial differences in the cost of equity capital. This has implications for financial theorists and analysts as well as corporate managers, since these professionals should think carefully about the rate or rates of growth they are using.

Finally, our results are only partially explained by and, in turn, only partially support the main theories of international business. The implication for academics is that more comprehensive and complete theories are needed.

Appendix:
Major Economic Events (1965–78)

The goal of this appendix is to show what major economic and political events took place during the period under study (1965-78). Rather than limiting ourselves to a strict ex post history of the period, there will be an assessment of past reports, which have tried to predict what possible developments were to take place in the near and distant future.

A very important factor that influences stock prices and therefore the cost of equity capital, earnings-price ratios, and betas is naturally inflation. The inflationary bout of the 1970s began with the U.S. military intervention in Vietnam in 1965. The inflation rate, which was 1.5 percent before that, doubled to 3 percent in 1966 and 1967, then redoubled to 6 percent in 1969 and 1970. Helped by a lull in economic activity and the imposition of direct wage and price controls, the inflation rate fell to the 3.5 percent level during 1972. However, at the end of 1972, prices began to accelerate. In 1974, the rate of inflation had reached 12 percent (Solomon 1975, pp. 19-20).

Before proceeding any further, it would be useful to explain in some detail the relationship between inflation and share prices up to 1968 and from then until the late 1970s.

From 1949 to the end of 1968, a period of relatively steady inflation, the Standard and Poor's Index of 500 common stock prices (S & P 500) increased sevenfold, from 15.2 to 106.5. If this increase is adjusted for inflation the real increase was 4.5 times. The false conclusion that people reached in general was that common stock prices would continue to rise, providing investors with a continuous hedge against whatever inflation might occur. A corollary of this false argument was that there was a shortage of good stocks relative to the rising demands for stocks. Between 1949 and 1968, common stock held by pension funds and other institutional investors increased from $13 billion to $220 billion. Even when one looks solely at the real increase, it is still a formidable one. This created the myth that inflation was "good" for stock prices and that the continuous pressure of institutional buying would keep stock prices rising. However, these suppositions were seriously doubted at the end of 1965 when the present inflationary round began. They were totally discarded due to the course of events that began at the end of 1968. The S & P 500 stock price index, which averaged 106.5 during December 1968, averaged 69.4 during October 1974. If we adjust for inflation, the price of stocks had fallen by almost 50 percent. Since the end of 1968, inflation has clearly been "bad" for stock prices. Stocks have provided a poorer hedge against inflation than almost any other kind of investment. Moreover, the continuing purchases of stocks by institutional investors did not help the stock prices at all (Solomon 1975, pp. 107-10).

The reason behind those changes could be that those people who invest in bonds may have a different expectation than those who buy stocks, the latter being mainly managers of pension funds and other institutions. Unlike the bond buyers who expect a high inflation rate to continue, stock buyers believe that the inflationary period is bound to end.

Sharpe (1978, p. 173) and Lintner (1975) also reach the conclusion that U.S. common stock prices have generally disproved the thesis that stocks are adequate hedges against price-level changes on a month-to-month or even year-to-year basis. Both nominal and real returns were negatively related to the rate of inflation, both expected and actual, when relatively short holding periods were compared.

Another point that is very important in analyzing the systematic risk or beta is whether or not the business cycle in the United States acted in unison with cycles in Europe or the rest of the world. In the latest recession, which began in October 1973, the level of activity in most of the major free world economies, where most of the U.S. foreign direct investment is located, moved down together with the U.S. economy under the common pressure of a sharp cutback in petroleum supplies and the very large increase in petroleum prices (Solomon 1975, p. 81). This, of course, greatly reduced or totally eliminated the beneficial effects of international diversification. Thus, the betas of multinational firms should have increased in relation to those of domestic firms and they did.

Compared to the rest of the 1960s, 1964 could definitely be considered a good year. The Dow Jones Industrial Average was 874.13 at the end of 1964, which was up 111.18 points compared to a year before. (See Figure A.1 for the Dow Jones Averages from 1965 to 1977.) A seat sold for $230,000, the highest since 1933, and volume had been 1,236,600 shares, which was a record. At the end of 1964, the economy was in a good condition, having achieved a balance between growth and inflation. On the political side, there was a lull in the cold war, and Johnson became president with a wide margin of votes, thus having a strong mandate. The U.S. intervention in Vietnam had not reached the large scale it was to reach later in 1965. So, at the beginning of 1965, the economy looked buoyant (Sobel 1975, pp. 288-89). Despite a slight decline in the stock prices in June, the euphoria continued until the end of the year, when there was a massive escalation of U.S. forces in Vietnam. After that, while inflation began to accelerate, stock prices began to fall. As expressed before, this was not in line with what had happened during former inflationary periods. The decline in stock prices reached its nadir in October 1966, after which they began to rise again (Economic Indicators 1969, p. 34). During the year, mounting defense expenditures and an upward revision of business investment expenditures, together with the multiplier effects of large investments made before, were putting increasing pressures on capacity and prices (Economist Quarterly 1966b).

FIGURE A.1. Dow Jones Industrial Forty-Week Moving Average.

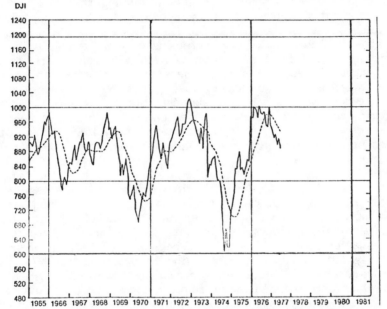

Source: Fogler, R. H. 1978. Analyzing the Stock Market: Statistical Evidence and Methodology, p. 153. Columbus, Ohio: Grid. Original Source: William Gordon, Gordon Associates, Miami Beach, Florida.

The economy's expansion slowed down again toward the end of 1966. The main reason for that was a large backing of unsold inventory. Moreover, the capital budgets of the business sector suffered a sharp reduction while consumption slackened. Only government spending was on the upsurge (Economist Quarterly 1967a). The slower growth removed the immediate threat of inflation. Still, upward wage demands could change that picture. The monetary authorities were pursuing a more expansionary policy, and interest rates were coming down (Economist Quarterly 1967a). The inventory surplus problem persisted in the first quarter of 1967, and the GNP did not increase in real terms. On the other hand, a recession was not likely, and an acceleration of final sales was expected toward the end of the year. Business fixed investment kept increasing (Economist Quarterly 1967b). At the end of 1967, the economy did pick up again after an inventory rundown. However, the war in Vietnam, continued social discontent, inflation, and uncertainty about the economy's future were sources of worry for the public and the investors (Economist Quarterly 1968).

The end of 1968 and the beginning of 1969 showed a slower expansion of the U.S. economy. Since inflation was the major problem, the Nixon administration was trying to resolve the dilemma of fighting against inflation without pushing the economy into a recession (Economist Quarterly 1969a).

In October 1968, there was a general feeling that the war in Vietnam might slow down. Even though there was no peace, prices and volume rose at the NYSE. The Dow Jones Industrial Average was above the 950 mark after increasing by more than 100 points since February. After the election of Richard Nixon as president, the market peaked at 985.21 on December 3 after which prices began to fall until the middle of 1970 (Sobel 1975, pp. 320-21). A major reason for this was the administration's tight money policy that tried to stem inflation. The discount rate, which had been 4 percent in October 1967, was 5.5 percent in early 1969 and went to 6 percent in April, which was a mark not seen since 1929 (Sobel 1975, pp. 320-21).

The economic and political uncertainties made the small investors nervous, while the institutions (insurance and investment companies, pension funds, nonprofit institutions, common trust funds, mutual savings banks, etc.) became wary (Sobel 1975, pp. 320-21). In any case, investors were expecting a mild and short recession for the latter part of 1969 and the beginning of 1970 (Economist Quarterly 1969b). Actually, during the first quarter of 1970, the aftertax profits of manufacturing corporations were down 13 percent, which corresponded to the same period of the previous year. This was the main reason that Dow Jones fell below the 700 mark (Economist Quarterly 1970a). The high-technology issues suffered the most. On May 26, the Dow Jones fell by 10.20 points and closed at 631.6 points, which was even below where it had been when Kennedy was inaugurated ten years earlier. Sobel thinks that it could have been worse had it not been for a generation of investors who had never known real panic before. They had become used to the idea that protection was at hand from the government and so did not give the matter serious consideration (Sobel 1975, p. 324). Unlike the quasi-paranoid investors of the late 1920s and the late 1930s, they had a high confidence in government and business institutions (Sobel 1975, p. 324). Thus it came as no surprise to see the stocks stabilizing in June and then rallying in July 1970. On August 28, the Dow Jones closed at 765.81 after rising more than 130 points in three months. According to Sobel (1975, p. 325), "It was an 'on-off market' with investors' moods switching from extreme bullishness to gloomy bearishness suddenly without stopping in between, and in each case ignoring contrary evidence on the other side." During this second half of 1970 when stock prices recovered, wholesale prices slowed down for a while. The government was expected to produce a deficit budget for 1971-72. Money became easier and interest rates had fallen. The Dow Jones exceeded 800 in December and Wall Street was optimistic (Economist Quarterly 1970b). In the end, it was calculated that GNP had fallen by 0.4 percent in 1970 (Economist Quarterly 1971a).

Inflationary forces remained strong at the beginning of 1971. The government acted to moderate steel prices, making a strike very probable (Economist Quarterly 1971a). GNP rose at an annual rate of 7.1 percent in the first quarter of 1971. This was a marked improvement over 1970. Industrial production and inventories were growing only slowly. The growth was led by nondurables (mainly food products). The general feeling was that the battle against inflation was to be a long one. While the money supply was rising fast, corporate profits were recovering (Economist Quarterly 1971b). On August 15, 1971, the president announced the following crisis measures against persistently high unemployment and inflation: a 90-day wage and prize freeze, an investment tax credit, the abolition of the excise duty on cars, acceleration of income tax concessions, a number of expenditure cuts, and a suspension of the dollar's convertibility to gold. There was also to be a 10 percent surcharge on most imports and a 10 percent cut in foreign aid. GNP grew at an annualized rate of 4.8 percent in real terms during the second quarter of 1971 (Economist Quarterly 1971c). GNP growth slowed to 3.9 percent in the third quarter during which the inflationary trend slowed down. The stock market recovered (Economist Quarterly 1971d); real growth for the whole of 1971 was 2.7 percent after a revision of figures (Economist Quarterly 1972a).

Stock prices rose to a high level in the summer of 1972. The Dow Jones, which had fallen to 889.15 on January 26, rose to close at 973.51 on August 14 before Election Day, which should normally have been full of uncertainty. In 1972, however, because of his antibusiness views, the presidential candidate George McGovern had little prospects of winning the election. If McGovern had been elected, it is generally believed that stock prices would have fallen sharply. But since the prospects of his electoral victory were extremely slim, the investors were not affected. In any case, when the other candidate, Richard Nixon, won a landslide victory, prices rose and exceeded the 1,000 mark to reach 1,036.27 on December 11 before settling down toward the end of the month. Then, when the Vietnam War ended, stock prices rose pushing the Dow Jones to a peak of 1,051.70 on January 11, 1973 (Sobel 1975, p. 362). A November 1972 survey put business plant and equipment expenditure 9 percent up in 1972 and forecasted a further large increase for the first half of 1973, especially in manufacturing. The annualized increase in prices was 3.8 percent a year during September, October, and November 1972 with food prices pushing up the rate

(Economist Quarterly 1972b). Although the administration had pledged to keep inflation under control, the cost of living was still increasing rapidly. Interest rates were also increasing but they did not seem to have an influence on prices as yet (Sobel 1975, p. 363).

Then, in 1973, there was the famous Watergate scandal. As this event and the trials dominated the newspaper headlines, public confidence in President Nixon declined rapidly. In addition to substantial inflation, high interest rates, and the president's impeachment because of the Watergate affair, meat shortages arose in the summer of 1973, while there was a fuel shortage in the fall (Sobel 1975, p. 363). Meat shortages were due to the price freezes, which aimed to cut the rate of inflation, while the fuel shortage was because of the Arab oil boycott, which in turn arose due to the United States' massive military help to Israel during its October 1973 war against Syria and Egypt.

By the end of 1973, "serious and sober" people began to wonder whether the world was not on the edge of a recession that would dwarf that of 1929-33. Corporate profits were excellent in 1972 and 1973 but, in the end, several of the speculative shares lost value, and that added further worries about the general state of the economy. As Sobel explains it:

> The illegal involvement of some businesses and businessmen in the Nixon campaign, combined with the windfall profits of major petroleum companies after the Arab oil boycott, added to the general woes caused by inflation and high interest rates. The economic and political agonies the nation underwent in 1973 and early 1974 were scarcely less traumatic than those suffered during the Vietnam War. Then came the impeachment debates followed by Nixon's resignation and the uncertain early days of President Ford. . . . The economy began to decline in the second half of 1974, as antiinflationary programs had their impact. By early 1975, it was evident that the nation had entered its worst recession since the 1930s and the future appeared bleak (Sobel 1975, p. 363).

All these events and feelings found their reflections on stock prices. The Dow Jones fell in 1973 and then prices collapsed in 1974. Unlike 1929, which had witnessed a sudden crash, 1974 consisted of a series of sharp declines followed by weak recoveries. The Dow Jones was 851.90 on August 22, 1973. It rose to 987.06 by October 26, and then fell to 788.31 on December 12, 1973 (Sobel 1975, pp. 363-64). All these movements shattered the confidence of investors, who began to desert the stock market. Many started to speculate in gold or bought commercial papers. Also because of rising inflation, people had to spend more and thus to save less since, in general, wages did not keep up with inflation.

Unlike the great depression of 1929-33, 1974 was a year of stagflation, that is, a combination of inflation and stagnation. Moreover, all stocks did not fall equally. A large group of well-established growth issues like Xerox, Polaroid, American Telephone and Telegraph, Pfizer, Kresge, etc. were bought by gigantic funds and other institutional investors. The latter not only clung to the shares of these companies but also supported their prices by buying them whenever they began to fall. This situation, which kept the stock prices of certain companies high in relation to others, was called the "Two-Tier Market." Naturally, this artificial phenomenon could not have gone on forever, and the collapse came in late 1973 and continued in 1974. The mutual funds, which owned large bulks of these issues, declined drastically. For instance, Morgan Guaranty controlled over $2 billion of IBM alone (Sobel 1975, pp. 364-65). The massive losses incurred by funds led individual investors to sell their shares. This led to a further decline in prices. Finally, fearing both a continued decline in stock prices and widespread redemptions, many of the mutual funds withdrew from the stock market and put their money in commercial paper and treasury notes (Sobel 1975, p. 366). This further depressed stock prices. At one point in 1974, there was a hope that institutional investors would come back to buy stocks again, but this did not materialize (Sobel 1975, p. 366). Instead, prices fell and rose with spurts, and the general trend was dipping sharply downward.

It was later calculated that real GNP growth was 5.9 percent in 1973 (Economist Quarterly 1974a). It could have been higher had it not been for the oil shortages and the consequent decline in the car industry. Over the last quarter of 1973, consumer spending declined by an annual rate of 2.4 percent (Economist Quarterly 1974a).

At the beginning of 1974, wage and price controls were expected to end in all industries except health and petroleum products by April 30. As controls were lifted, consumer prices were jolting upward. Wholesale prices showed a one-month jump of 7.7 percent in February. Farm product prices went up by 11.7 percent during the first quarter of 1974 (Economist Quarterly 1974a).

During the same period, GNP declined by 6.3 percent as personal consumption expenditure, the prime component of GNP, declined for the second consecutive quarter (Economist Quarterly 1974b). Real personal spending diminished by 2.8 percent in the first quarter, while spending on services continued to expand. Dividend growth decelerated substantially, and real disposable incomes were declining by over 6 percent at an annual rate. Retail sales growth was hampered by poor car sales, but there were expectations for improvements. The Federal Reserve was continuing its tight monetary policy to prevent inflation (Economist Quarterly 1974b).

Real GNP declined by 1.2 percent in the second quarter of 1974, but real personal consumption was rising a little. The rapid expansion in growth of new orders made a gain in real industrial output by the end of the year a possibility (Economist Quarterly 1974c). Consumer spending on durable goods, particularly new car sales, pushed up real spending despite the poor showing for nondurables and services. A high level of capital expenditures was still forecast for the end of 1974 (Economist Quarterly 1974c).

Real GNP fell by 2.1 percent in the third quarter of 1974. Retail sales fell since September even by current prices, led by a decrease in automobile sales. Business expectations for 1975 suggested a drop of 3 to 4 percent in real investments (Economist Quarterly 1974d).

The GNP increased by 3.3 percent annually at current prices during the fourth quarter of 1974, but at constant prices it was an annual decline of 9.1 percent. GNP in 1974 was 2.2 percent lower than in 1973 in real terms (Economist Quarterly 1975a). Industrial production decreased by 3.6 percent in January and 8.9 percent in the three months since October 1974. New orders of durable goods slumped in December 1974 and continued to fall in January 1975 (Economist Quarterly 1975a).

There was an 11.3 percent real decrease in the GNP during the first quarter of 1975. Industrial production was 12.4 percent lower in April compared to the same period of the previous year (Economist Quarterly 1975b).

The outlook for cars, business equipment, and steel was gloomy. Consumer prices in April 1975 were up 10.2 percent compared with the previous year. Pretax profits fell by 24 percent between the last quarter of 1974 and the first of 1975, but the stock market continued recovering, and it was expected that the GNP growth rate could reach 7 percent by the first quarter of 1976 (Economist Quarterly 1975b).

The real GNP growth for the third quarter of 1975 was a 13.2 percent annual rate. The rise in industrial production was flattening out after a notable rebound in consumer durables. It was the spending on cars that brought about the fast GNP growth in the third quarter (Economist Quarterly 1975c).

The GNP real growth rate fell back to 4.9 percent in the fourth quarter of 1975. Industrial production grew at an annual rate of 8.8 percent during December, January, and February. Although inventory-to-sales ratios were falling, depressed business capital spending was unlikely to recover much in 1976. The recovery of profits and share prices continued up to February (Economist Quarterly 1976a).

In spite of a smaller increase in final sales, a shift to inventory accumulation brought about a fast real annual GNP growth rate of 8.5 (later revised at 9.2) percent in the first quarter of 1976. The two most important items leading to a rapid increase in consumer spending were food and cars. Due to more expensive oil and food prices, consumer prices rose by 0.6 percent in May 1976 (Economist Quarterly 1976b).

In the second quarter of 1976, real GNP grew at an annual rate of 4.4 percent. Accumulated inventory decreased due to increased final sales. Inflation seemed to be rising (Economist Quarterly 1976c).

If Jimmy Carter, the new president, were to provide some stimulus to the economy on taking office, GNP was expected to grow by about 5 percent in real terms between 1976 and 1977 (Economist Quarterly 1976d). Real GNP growth was an annual 3.8 percent in the third quarter of 1976. Industrial production declined during September and October due to low retail sales and an involuntary buildup in inventories, which led to reduced ordering rates (Economist Quarterly 1976d).

During the first quarter of 1977, Wall Street was more pessimistic than President Carter about inflation, as it feared that price controls or tighter monetary policy might follow. However, it was also thought that the rise in the inflation rate and interest rates could be sufficiently moderate to allow the upward trend to continue early in 1978 (Economist Quarterly 1977a). For 1977, prospects seemed to be more solid. After the poor first quarter growth, which was affected by bad weather, a high 9.5 percent annual growth was expected in the second quarter. An inventory buildup would help this. Except for fuel products, industrial production fell in January almost across the board but recovered in February, when orders for capital goods were still lagging but were expected to pick up in the wake of large orders for consumer durable products (Economist Quarterly 1977a).

GNP was expected to rise by 5.3 percent in 1977 despite decreasing consumer expenditures resulting from higher savings and taxes. This growth was expected to slow down in the second half of the year with housing and business capital as strong features (Economist Quarterly 1977b). The first quarter GNP growth rate went up to 6.9 percent due to a recovery in stockbuilding. New orders for goods looked healthy; during the first five months, retail prices increased by 9.5 percent but were expected to slow down (Economist Quarterly 1977b).

Slower growth rather than recession was the expectation for 1978. Government spending, especially by the states and local governments, was to be an expansionary factor; GNP was expected to rise by 5 percent for 1977 and just under 5 percent for the first half of 1978. Wholesale prices fell because of lower farm prices, while the rate of retail price inflation moderated (Economist Quarterly 1977c).

The real GNP growth rate of the fourth quarter in 1977 was not expected to exceed 4.9 percent despite the buoyancy of the economy. This was due to reduced stockholding. Investments were expected to increase once policy uncertainties were eliminated. A real GNP growth rate of 4.6 percent was forecast for 1978. Wholesale prices began to increase faster even though retail prices were still not affected by October 1977 (Economist Quarterly 1977d).

An unusually hard winter in the early months of 1978 depressed economic activity, especially the construction and retail sectors. However, considerable improvement was expected in the second and third quarters of 1978, when there would be a high level of activity to make up for the time lost during the first quarter. Industrial production slowed down partly because of the previous high buildup of inventories held by retailers. The influence of rising wholesale prices was also felt in consumer prices, which also rose during the first quarter of 1978 (Economist Quarterly 1978a).

Bad weather, the coal strike, and a weakening underlying trend reduced real GNP growth to zero in the first quarter of 1978. However, industrial production came back strongly in the March-May period, led by business equipment (Economist Quarterly 1978b). There was a surge in retail sales in March and April, but they dropped back in May. Increased savings and worse inflation caused a fall in consumer spending (Economist Quarterly 1978b).

In the above explanations of major economic events, the relations of some of the events to the results of our test have been indicated. Some more explanations have already been given in the three chapters dealing with the results and the comparison of forward-looking and historical growth rates. However, it would be appropriate to explain the phenomenon of stagflation and virtually synchronized economic cycles in major industrialized countries after 1973. This should be of essential importance when explaining the results of the betas.

Unlike the inflationary periods during the 1940s and 1950s, inflation in the 1970s has affected the quasi-totality of the industrialized countries. Consequently, multinational corporations have had less possibilities of fighting against inflation by shifting investments or purchases from one set of countries to another. During previous inflationary bouts, many multinational firms had sought to keep their costs at a steady level by buying their raw materials or component parts from countries that had a lower rate of inflation and/or lower prices. Thus, by increasing their purchases of Japanese steel, U.S. and European firms had attempted to reduce their costs by finding competitive suppliers.

Moreover, during the entire period after World War II, the business cycles of the major industrialized countries did not coincide with one another. This was a very important factor since it was beneficial for the international diversification of the multinational firms by reducing their systematic risks (betas). For instance, when industries were working at almost full capacity, thus resulting in higher prices in the United States, it was possible to find other industrialized countries with industries working at only partial capacity. This meant that the latter countries would sell their products at lower prices. Consequently, U.S. firms were able to get supplies at lower costs from other countries or from their sub-sidiaries. Obviously, this situation gave the U.S. multinational corporations a relative edge over the U.S. domestic firms. The former had wider possibilities of diversification and could reduce their global risk and stabilize their profits.

During the early 1970s, the demand of industrial products and then of raw materials increased in all industrialized countries and was often accompanied by factories working at full productive capacity. Price increases were rapidly felt; in numerous cases, the increase in the prices of raw materials during 1972 and 1973 alone exceeded those observed during the entire decade of the 1960s. Thus, the possibilities of escaping the negative aspects of inflation by diversifying sources of supplies became a virtual impossibility for multinational firms. Beginning from 1973, the general demand diminished substantially despite a persisting inflation. Firms had to face the combined effect of cost increases and reduced demand. This situation, which spread to all the industrialized Western countries, diminished the benefits of international diversification.

Bibliography

Aggarwal, R. 1979. "Multinationality and Stock Market Valuation: An Empirical Study of U.S. Markets and Companies." Management International Review 19: 5-21.

Ajami, R. A. 1979. Arab Responses to the Multinationals. New York: Praeger.

Aliber, R. Z. 1970. "A Theory of Direct Foreign Investment." In The International Corporation, edited by C. P. Kindleberger. Cambridge, Mass.: M.I.T. Press.

Alpander, G. Fall 1973. "Drift to Authoritarianism: The Changing Managerial Types of U.S. Executives Overseas." Journal of International Business Studies 4: 1-14.

Amling, F. 1978. Investments: An Introduction to Analysis and Management. Englewood Cliffs, N.J.: Prentice-Hall.

Baldwin, R. E. 1971. "Determinants of the Commodity Structure of the U.S. Trade." American Economic Review 61: 126-46.

Bernhard, A. 1978. "How to Invest in Common Stocks with the Aid of Value Line Investment Survey." Value Line Investment Survey 10-42.

Brandt, W. K., and J. M. Hulbert. 1976. "Patterns of Communications in the Multinational Corporation: An Empirical Study." Journal of International Business Studies 7-8, 57.

Brigham, E. F., and D. K. Shome. 1979. "Estimating the Market Risk Premium." Paper presented at the Conference on Financial Management of Corporate Resource Allocations, The Netherlands School of Business, Breukelen.

Brown, L. D., and M. S. Rozeff. 1978. "The Superiority of Analyst Forecasts as Measures of Expectations: Evidence from Earnings." Journal of Finance 33: 1-16.

Bruck, N. K., and F. A. Lees. April 1968. "Foreign Investment, Capital Controls, and the Balance of Payments." The Bulletin (New York University) nos. 48-49: 69-102.

Caves, R. E. 1969. "International Corporations: The Industrial Economics of Foreign Investment." In Royer Lectures, p. 5. Berkeley: University of California Press.

Chung, W. K. March 1978. "Sales by Majority-Owned Foreign Affiliates of U.S. Companies, 1976." Survey of Current Business 58: 31-40.

Clapham, M. 1975. Multinational Enterprise and the Nation States. London: Athlone Press.

Cooper, R. N. 1968. The Economics of Interdependence: Economic Policy in the Atlantic Community. New York: McGraw-Hill.

D'Ambrosio, C. A. 1976. Principles of Modern Investments. Chicago: Science Research Associates.

Douglass, M. E. December 1976. "Relating Education to Entrepreneurial Success." Business Horizons 41.

Economic Indicators. March 1969. Washington, D.C.: U.S. Government Printing Office. 34.

_____. March 1979. Washington, D.C.: U.S. Government Printing Office. 31.

The Economist. September 19, 1977. "A Survey of American Companies in Europe." London.

_____. June 23, 1979. "A Survey of Foreign Investment in Asia." London.

The Economist Intelligence Unit Quarterly Economic Review: U.S.A. March 1966a. London.

_____. June 1966b. London.

_____. March 1967a. London.

_____. June 1967b. London.

_____. December 1968. London.

_____. March 1969a. London.

_____. September 1969b. London.

_____. June 1970a. London.

_____. December 1970b. London.

_____. March 1971a. London.

The Economist Intelligence Unit Quarterly Economic Review: U.S.A.
June 1971b. London.

_____. September 1971c. London.

_____. December 1971d. London.

_____. March 1972a. London.

_____. December 1972b. London.

_____. March 1974a. London.

_____. June 1974b. London.

_____. September 1974c. London.

_____. December 1974d. London.

_____. March 1975a. London.

The Economist Intelligence Unit Quarterly Economic Review: U.S.A.
June 1975b. London.

_____. December 1975c. London.

_____. March 1976a. London.

_____. June 1976b. London.

_____. September 1976c. London.

_____. December 1976d. London.

_____. March 1977a. London.

_____. June 1977b. London.

_____. September 1977c. London.

_____. December 1977d. London.

The Economist Intelligence Unit Quarterly Economic Review: U.S.A. March 1978a. London.

_____. June 1978b. London.

Fatemi, N., T. de Saint-Phalle, and G. Keefe. 1963. The Dollar Crisis. Rutherford, N.J.: Fairleigh Dickinson Press.

Fatemi, N., G. Williams, and T. de Saint-Phalle. 1976. Multinational Corporations: Problems and Prospects. New York: A. S. Barnes.

Fayerweather, J. 1969. International Business Management: A Conceptual Framework, pp. 15-55. New York: McGraw-Hill.

Fisher, L., and J. H. Lorie. 1966. "Rates of Return on Investments in Common Stocks." In Frontiers of Investment Analysis, edited by E. G. Frederickson. Scranton, Pa.: International Textbook.

Fogler, R. H. 1978. Analyzing the Stock Market: Statistical Evidence and Methodology. Columbus, Ohio: Grid.

Frank, I. 1980. Foreign Enterprise in Developing Countries. Baltimore: Johns Hopkins University Press.

Freidlin, N. J., and L. A. Lupo. November 1972. "U.S. Direct Investments Abroad in 1971." Survey of Current Business 52: 21-34.

Geyikdagi, Y. 1980. "Multinationality and Stock Market Valuation: An Empirical Study of U.S. Markets and Companies – A Comment." Management International Review 20: 122-23.

Gordon, M. 1962. The Investment, Financing and Valuation of the Corporation. Homewood, Ill.: Richard D. Irwin.

Graham, B., D. L. Dodd, and S. Cottle. 1962. Security Analysis. New York: McGraw-Hill.

Gruber, W., D. Mehta, and R. Vernon. 1967. "The Research and Development Factor in International Trade and International Investment of U.S. Industry." Journal of Political Economy 75: 20-37.

Hanson, J.S. November-December 1975. "Transfer Pricing in the Multinational Corporation: A Critical Appraisal." World Development vol. 3, nos. 11, 12.

Hill, R. 1976. "The Benefits of an International Advisory Board." International Management 15: 28-31.

Hirsch, S., and B. Lev. August 1971. "Sales Stabilization through Export Diversification." Review of Economics and Statistics 53: 270-77.

Ibbotson, R. G., and R. A. Sinquefield. 1976a. "Stocks, Bonds, Bills, and Inflation: Year by Year Historical Returns (1926-74)." The Journal of Business 49: 11-47.

_____. 1976b. "Stocks, Bonds, Bills, and Inflation: Simulation of the Future (1976-2000)." Journal of Business 49: 313-38.

Kohers, T. 1971. "A Comparison of Financial Performance between U.S. Multinational Corporations and U.S. Domestic Corporations." Ph.D. dissertation, University of Oregon.

_____. 1975. "The Effect of Multinational Operations on the Cost of Equity Capital of U.S. Corporations: An Empirical Study." Management International Review 15: 121-24.

Kozlow, R., J. Rutter, and P. Walker. August 1978. "U.S. Direct Investment Abroad in 1977." Survey of Current Business 58: 16-38.

Lamfalussy, A. 1961. Investment and Growth in Mature Economies. Oxford: Basil Blackwell & Mott.

Leon, P. 1977. Histoire economique et sociale du monde: 1947 a nos jours. Paris: Armand Colin.

Levis, M. 1979. "Does Political Instability in Developing Countries Affect Foreign Investment Flow? An Empirical Examination." Management International Review 19: 59-68.

Levy, H., and M. Sarnat. 1970. "International Diversification of Investment Portfolios." American Economic Review 60: 668-75.

Lintner, J. May 1975. "Inflation and Security Returns." Journal of Finance 30: 259-80.

Lorange, P. 1976. A Framework for Strategic Planning in Multinational Corporations. Cambridge, Mass.: M.I.T. Press.

Lupo, L. A. September 1973. "U.S. Direct Investment Abroad in 1972." Survey of Current Business 53: 21-34.

Malkiel, B. G. 1979. "The Capital Formation Problem in the United States." The Journal of Finance 34: 297-300.

Markowitz, H. (1959). Portfolio Selection: Efficient Diversification of Investments. New York: John Wiley.

Meier, G. M. 1972. "Private Foreign Investment." In International Investment, edited by J. H. Dunning. Middlesex, England: Penguin Books.

Mendenhall, W., and J. E. Reinmuth. 1974. Statistics for Management and Economics. North Scituate, Mass.: Duxbury Press.

Oğuz, Y. 1976. Planli Dönemlerde Teknoloji. Ankara: T. C. Basbakanlik Devlet Planlama Teşkilati.

Penrose, E. 1971. "State and Multinational Enterprise in Less-Developed Countries." In The Multinational Enterprise, edited by J. Dunning. London: George Allen & Unwin.

Phatak, Q. V. 1971. Evolution of World Enterprise. New York: American Management.

Pras, B. 1980. La firme multinationale face au risque. Paris: Presses Universitaries de France.

Price Waterhouse Information Guide for Doing Business in ... (various dates and countries). New York.

Reuber, G. L. 1973. Private Foreign Investment in Development. Oxford: Clarendon Press.

Rugman, A. 1979. International Diversification and the Multinational Enterprise. Lexington, Mass.: Lexington.

Sadchev, J. October 1977. "Dilution of Ownership in Multinational Concerns." Long Range Planning 10: 33-39.

Sakr, N. October 1977. "Syria Meets Foreign Investors Halfway." The Middle East 36, 66.

Salama, P. April-June 1978. "Specificité de l'internationalisation du capital en Amérique latine." Revue Tiers Monde 19: 259-98.

Scholl, R. B. August 1974. "The International Investment Position of the United States: Developments in 1973." Survey of Current Businesses 54: 1-6.

Servan-Schreiber, J. J. 1967. Le Defi Americain. Paris: Denoel.

Sharpe, W. 1978. Investments. Englewood Cliffs, N.J.: Prentice-Hall.

Singer, H. W., and J. A. Ansari. 1977. Rich and Poor Countries. London: George Allen & Unwin.

Sobel, R. 1975. A History of the New York Stock Exchange: 1935-1975. New York: Weybright and Talley.

Solomon, E. 1975. The Anxious Economy. San Francisco: W. H. Freeman.

Spiegel, M. R. 1961. Theory and Problems of Statistics. New York: Schaum.

Standard & Poor's. Industry Surveys (various issues) New York.

U.S. Department of Commerce. 1972. Policy Aspects of Foreign Investment by U.S. Multinational Corporations. Washington, D.C.: U.S. Government Printing Office.

_____. U.S. Industrial Outlook (various issues) Washington, D.C.: U.S. Government Printing Office.

Value Line Investment Survey. (various issues) New York.

Van Horne, J. C., C. R. Dipchand, and J. R. Hanrahan. 1977. Financial Management and Policy. Canadian 4th ed. Scarborough, Ontario: Prentice-Hall of Canada.

Vernon, R. 1971. Sovereignty at Bay. New York: Basic Books.

_____. 1966. "International Investment and International Trade in the Product Cycle." Quarterly Journal of Economics 80: 190-207.

Weller, D. October 1973. "Can A Ph.D. Make It as a Vice President?" Master in Business Administration 25-26, 36.

Weston, J. J. 1966. The Scope and Methodology of Finance. Englewood Cliffs, N.J.: Prentice-Hall.

Weston, J.F., and E. F. Brigham. 1975. Managerial Finance. Hinsdale, Ill.: Holt, Rinehart & Winston.

_____. 1978. Managerial Finance. Hinsdale, Ill.: Dryden Press.

Widing, J. W. 1973. "Reorganizing Your Worldwide Business." Harvard Business Review 51: 153-60.

Wilkins, M. 1974. The Maturing of Multinational Enterprise: American Business Abroad from 1914 to 1970. Cambridge, Mass.: Harvard University Press.

Wood, G. E., and N. A. Jianakoplos. 1979. "Coordinated International Economic Expansion: Are Convoys or Locomotives the Answer?" In International Business - 1979. A Selection of Current Readings, edited by D. A. Anderson, M. Luqmani, and Z. A. Quraeshi, pp. 47-55. East Lansing: Michigan State University Press.

Index

About the Author

MEHMET YASAR GEYIKDAGI is a consultant in finance, international business, and economics. He has taught at several universities in Turkey and North America.

Dr. Geyikdagi has published in various fields and holds a license from the Ankara Academy (Turkey), an M.B.A. from Columbia University (New York), an M.A. from McGill University (Montreal) and a Ph.D. from the University of Bath (England).